# Proleptic Pedagogy

# Proleptic Pedagogy

Theological Education Anticipating the Future

Edited by **Sondra Higgins Matthaei**
and **Nancy R. Howell**

CASCADE *Books* • Eugene, Oregon

PROLEPTIC PEDAGOGY
Theological Education Anticipating the Future

Copyright © 2014 Wipf and Stock Publishers. All rights reserved. Except for brief quotations in critical publications or reviews, no part of this book may be reproduced in any manner without prior written permission from the publisher. Write: Permissions, Wipf and Stock Publishers, 199 W. 8th Ave., Suite 3, Eugene, OR 97401.

Cascade Books
An Imprint of Wipf and Stock Publishers
199 W. 8th Ave., Suite 3
Eugene, OR 97401

www.wipfandstock.com

ISBN 13: 978-1-62032-438-7

*Cataloging-in-Publication data:*

Proleptic pedagogy : theological education anticipating the future / edited by Sondra Higgins Matthaei and Nancy R. Howell.

xii + 158 p. ; 23 cm. Includes bibliographical references and index.

ISBN 13: 978-1-62032-438-7

1. Teaching—Religious aspects—Christianity. 2. Theology—Study and teaching. 3. Education (Christian theology). I. Matthaei, Sondra Higgins. II. Howell, Nancy R., 1953–. III. Title.

BV1610 P75 2014

Manufactured in the U.S.A.

# Contents

*List of Contributors* | *vii*

1 Proleptic Pedagogy, Transition, and Teaching toward the Future: An Introduction | 1
   *Nancy R. Howell*

2 Proleptic Pedagogy, Pluralism, and Pedagogical Agility | 8
   *Nancy R. Howell*

3 From Objectifying to Contemplating the Other: An Incarnational Approach to Pedagogy in Theological Education | 29
   *Robert Martin*

4 Student Formation through Experiential and Transformative Learning: Pedagogical Insights from/for Contextual Education | 55
   *James M. Brandt*

5 Immediacy: The Intersection of Technological and Face-to-face Modalities in Educating a Younger Generation | 70
   *Claire Annelise Smith*

6 Teaching Integrative Theological Reflection as a Way of Life | 92
   *Nancy R. Howell and F. Douglas Powe Jr.*

7 Pedagogical Issues in Theological Education for Diverse Peoples and Divergent Thinkers | 111
   *Sondra Higgins Matthaei with Jami Moss*

8 Hip-Hop in the Classroom | 130
   *F. Douglas Powe Jr.*

   *Bibliography* | *143*

   *Index* | *151*

# Contributors

**James M. Brandt** is Professor of Historical Theology and Director of Contextual Education at Saint Paul School of Theology in Kansas City, Missouri. Brandt received his Ph.D. from the University of Chicago. His Master of Divinity degree was conferred by Luther Theological Seminary, and he is an ordained minister in the Evangelical Lutheran Church in America (ELCA).

Brandt brings two specialties to his teaching. One disciplinary area is historical theology and ethics, as well as church history. A second disciplinary specialty includes practical theology, contextual education, spirituality, and social ministry. His representative course offerings range from "19th Century Protestant Theology" and "Luther and Schleiermacher" to "Preparing for Local Ministries," "Ministry in Context," and an Immersion course in Guatemala.

Brandt's publications include a translation entitled *Schleiermacher's Christian Ethics: Selections* (2011) and a scholarly book entitled *All Things New: Reform of Church and Society in Schleiermacher's Christian Ethics* (2001).

**Nancy R. Howell** is Professor of Theology and Philosophy of Religion at Saint Paul School of Theology in Kansas City, Missouri (where she also served as Academic Dean and Interim Vice President for Academic Affairs and Dean). She has taught for the Kansas City University of Medicine and Biosciences, and prior to 1998, in the Department of Religion at Pacific Lutheran University. Her current teaching includes courses on Whiteheadian feminism, John B. Cobb Jr., and process theology, as well as science and religion, liberation theology, and systematic theology. Howell earned

*Contributors*

her Ph.D. in Religion (Philosophy of Religion and Theology) at Claremont Graduate School in 1991.

Howell has participated in the Center for Theology and the Natural Sciences course award program and received prizes for development of two courses integrating science and religion, as well as an Altruistic Love and Science course award in 2005. She was a participant in the American Academy of Religion/Lilly Teaching Workshop for Mid-Career Faculty in 1997–1998 and attended the Educating Clergy Conference (Wabash Center) in 2005. With colleague F. Douglas Powe Jr., she received a Theological Education Renewal Award (Yale Divinity School) in 2007. Howell completed her Certificate in Distance Education (Instructional Development and Facilitation) from Indiana University School of Continuing Studies in 2010.

Howell's publications construct theology at the intersection of process theology, women's theologies, liberation theologies, and biological sciences. *A Feminist Cosmology: Ecology, Solidarity, and Metaphysics* (Humanity Books, 2000) engages diverse women's voices in dialogue with process theology with "reverence for the diversity of relationships among women, the deep interdependence of humanity and the ecosystem, and ultimately the variety of theological perspectives relating the world to God" (from the cover). Working with editor in chief Wentzel van Huyssteen and associate editors Wesley Wildman and Niels Gregersen, Howell is associate editor for the *Encyclopedia of Science and Religion* (Macmillan, 2003). Working with Monica A. Coleman and Helene Tallon Russell, Howell edited and contributed to *Creating Women's Theology: A Movement Engaging Process Thought* (Pickwick, 2011)—a book devoted to documenting the dialogue between women scholars and the philosophies of Hartshorne and Whitehead. Howell has served as book review editor and guest editor of *Process Studies* (22:2). In addition, she serves or served on editorial boards for *Theology and Science, American Journal of Theology and Philosophy, Journal of Religion and Abuse, Journal of the American Academy of Religion,* and *Science and Spirit*. She has reviewed book and journal manuscripts for numerous publishers.

**Robert Martin** is the Lovett H. Weems Associate Professor of Church Leadership and Practical Theology at Saint Paul School of Theology. A native of Louisiana, he studied at Princeton Theological Seminary and Harvard Divinity School, and he taught for six years at Yale Divinity School.

Lately, Dr. Martin has focused his attention on orienting leadership and church life sacramentally. To that end he has published a number of essays which include: "Toward a Wesleyan Sacramental Ecclesiology," *Ecclesiology* 9 (2013) 19–38; "Leadership and Serendipitous Discipleship: A Case Study of Congregational Transformation," in *Redemptive Transformation in Practical Theology: Essays in Honor of James E. Loder, Jr.*, edited by Dana R. Wright and John D. Kuentzel (W. B. Eerdmans Publishers, 2004); "*Insisto Rector*: Provocative Play for Serious Leadership Learning," coauthored with Russell W. West, *Journal of Religious Leadership* 11 (2012): 33–64. Martin currently serves on the editorial board of the *Journal of Religious Leadership*.

Dr. Martin has also been writing on theological epistemology and education, selections of which include: *The Incarnate Ground of Christian Faith: Toward a Christian Theological Epistemology for the Educational Ministry of the Church*, (University Press of America, 1998); "'Mind the Gap': Closing the Distance between Theological Method, Theological Education, and Practical Theology for Religious Leadership" and "Dwelling in the Divine Life: The Transformative Dimension of Leadership and Practical Theology," in *Journal of Religious Leadership* 3/1–2 (2004); "Having Faith in Our Faith in God: Toward a Critical Realist Epistemology for Christian Education," *Religious Education* 96/2 (2001). He was on the editorial board of *Teaching Theology and Religion*, 2000–2004.

**Sondra Matthaei**, Professor of Christian Religious Education, has taught at Saint Paul School of Theology for twenty-five years in three degree programs: Master of Arts in Christian Ministry, Master of Divinity and Doctor of Ministry. Representative courses taught include "Faith Formation in the Wesleyan Tradition" (Doctor of Ministry), "Introduction to Ministry," "Spiritual Direction/Companionship," "Spiritual Formation and Mentoring Relations," and Native American immersions with the Pueblo Peoples and with the Plains Tribes. Dr. Matthaei is a diaconal minister in The United Methodist Church with twenty years of educational and program ministry experience in the local church.

Dr. Matthaei's primary area of scholarship is Christian faith development with a particular focus on the early Methodist movement and the implications for Christian faith formation in the church today. Two basic questions are the focus of her scholarship: How do persons become Christian? What is the church's role in making disciples?

Matthaei's publications include *Youth Ministry in a Technological Age*, co-editor with Dr. Claire A. Smith (XLibris, 2011; *Loving God, Loving Neighbor: Ministry with Searching Youth*, editor (XLibris, 2008); *Formation in Faith*:

*Contributors*

*The Congregational Ministry of Making Disciples* (Abingdon, 2008); *Making Disciples: Faith Formation in the Wesleyan Tradition* (Abingdon, 2000); and *Faith Matters: Faith-Mentoring in the Faith Community* (Trinity, 1996).

**Jami Moss** is a student in the Master of Divinity degree program at Saint Paul School of Theology. Moss, who is of Creek American Indian origin, is a licensed local pastor in the Oklahoma Indian Missionary Conference of The United Methodist Church, serving Lawrence Indian United Methodist Church in Lawrence, Kansas and Kansas City Native American Ministries.

**F. Douglas Powe Jr.** is the E. Stanley Jones Associate Professor of Evangelism at Saint Paul School of Theology in Kansas City, Missouri. He directs the Evangelism Specialization and co-directs the Black Church Studies Specialization. Dr. Powe received the Theology as a Way of Life teaching award from Yale University in 2007 for "Theology in Black and White" a class co-taught with Nancy R. Howell. He also received the Jaguar Teacher of the Year award from Spelman College in 2004. He continues to be innovative in the classroom by integrating various forms of media with a goal to create a transformative space.

A forerunner in African American evangelism, Dr. Powe's contributions to the field include: *New Wine, New Wineskins: How African American Congregations Can Reach New Generations* (Abingdon Press, 2012), *Transforming Evangelism: The Wesleyan Way of Sharing Faith*, co-authored with Henry H. Knight, III (Discipleship Resources, 2006), "Such A Great Cloud of Witnesses: Evangelistically Vital Churches," in *God Delivers Me: A Model from Strengthening the Black Church for the 21st Century* (Abingdon, 2008), "Hearing The Voice of Our Neighbor: A Voice From the Other Side," in *Loving God, Loving Neighbor: Ministry with Questioning Youth* (XLibris, 2008), "Emerging Possibilities for African-American Worship," in *Africana Worship* (Discipleship Resources, 2007), "Is Liberation the Starting Point for an African-American Theology of Evangelism?" (*Union Quarterly Review*).

Dr. Powe is making a contribution to African American theology and Methodist theology. His scholarship in this area includes: *Just Us or Justice?: Moving Toward a Pan-Methodist Theology* (Abingdon, 2009), "A Tragic-Liberation Model: Hurston's Perspective on Life and Systematic Evil," *Black Theology: An International Journal* (January 2007), "John Wesley's Call to Personal and Social Holiness," "John Wesley's Call to Be an 'Altogether

Christian,'" "John Wesley on Mutuality in Mission," *A Year with John Wesley and Our Methodist Values* (Discipleship Resources, 2008).

**Claire Annelise Smith** (Ph.D. Union Presbyterian Seminary) is Director of *youTheology* and Youth Ministry Specialist-in-Residence at Saint Paul School of Theology in Kansas City, Missouri. She is a member of the Religious Education Association and serves on the Board of the Association of Youth Ministry Educators. She also served for ten years as Youth Coordinator for the Guyana Congregational Union where she had responsibilities for planning, executing, and coordinating national and international programs with youth and Sunday schools.

Claire Smith has published devotional material, chapters and articles, and presented scholarly papers at professional meetings. She co-edited *Youth Ministry in a Technological Age* (XLibris, 2011), in which she has a chapter entitled, "To Follow Christ: Youth Ministry in a Technological Age."

She enjoys connecting with friends and writing inspirational poetry. Her passion is creating space so that people may know God more.

# I

## Proleptic Pedagogy, Transition, and Teaching toward the Future
*An Introduction*

Nancy R. Howell

Could we have imagined how much theological education would change over the last decade? Saint Paul School of Theology might be typical of many seminaries, and the shifting needs of students, classrooms, and the church have demanded constant revisions of the curriculum, course design, classroom technology, and pedagogical strategies. Saint Paul was founded fifty-something years ago, and for thirty years enjoyed a fairly constant faculty with residential students who shared a common mission and values, which enhanced the sense of community and engaged students in peace and justice work in the Kansas City community.

The scope of change is remarkable. The faculty no longer includes the founding and shaping scholars who formed the seminary's identity. Students commute from Iowa, Nebraska, Kansas, and Missouri, and because Saint Paul added a second campus in Oklahoma City, the commuters travel from other states and across two campus locations. The student body grows ever more diverse, not only by geography, but also in terms of theology, denomination, race/ethnicity, nationality, age, and gendered and sexual identities—and we have learned to be more attentive to subtleties of learning styles and disabilities. From humble beginnings in classroom technology, faculty develop complexes of technology ranging from the necessary videoconferences connecting two campuses to challenging course management software, which bridge the geographical distances of commuting students and enhance resources, media, and classroom learning communities. Courses are delivered in face-to-face, hybrid, and videoconference modes with attention to how active learning and transformative pedagogies affect student professional formation. Building a sense of community beyond the earlier residential student life, worship, and community meals requires skills never imagined prior to the availability of technology. While demands have increased, financial resources have become more limited in recent difficult economic times, and our survival strategy entails the challenge and promise of leaving the Kansas City campus and entering collaboration with Church of the Resurrection in Kansas.

Saint Paul is not alone in its work to negotiate changes, and Dan Aleshire's plenary address to the 2010 Biennial Meeting of the Association of Theological Schools emphasized just how dramatic the changes are.[1] Aleshire said what many seminary faculties felt: "The change has been rapid and ubiquitous, and ATS schools have been affected by the scope and the pace."[2] No aspect of our work is untouched by the changes in religion, higher education, and students. Theological education is affected by religion in North America as denominations are structurally less central to Christian identity as religious participation and preference change generationally.[3] Additionally, Christianity is contextualized by the global multifaith context and religious pluralism.[4] Aleshire proposed that theological education needs three broad responses to change in North American religion. First, the seminary curriculum must take account of non-Christian religious affiliation, as well as decreasing commitment to religious affiliation.[5] Second, theological education must have broader options in degree programs, educational models, and leadership development.[6] Third, theological education must respond by diversifying educational practices through attention

---

1. Aleshire, "The Future Has Arrived."
2. Ibid., 1.
3. Ibid., 2.
4. Ibid., 3.
5. Ibid., 5.
6. Ibid., 7.

to higher education conventions, alternative professional formation options, and educational technology.[7] Aleshire developed the three responses in light of the following statement:

> What are the responses that will make theological schools as effective in the future as they have been in the past? Because change has been so massive, theological schools need to focus their attention on the areas where their efforts can have greatest impact: North American religion and the practices of theological education. Religion is awash with fundamental change, but it remains to be seen how faithfully theological schools will change.[8]

Aleshire's plenary captured the urgency of change in theological education, and he called for responsive (rather than reactive) change.

Saint Paul School of Theology felt the tide of change within our own walls, and the Wabash Center deserves our great appreciation for providing resources to help us with pedagogical development from 2007 through 2010. The Wabash Center funded a project that the Saint Paul faculty called "Proleptic Pedagogy: Teaching from the Future to Distance, Disability, and Race," which attended to three distinct pedagogical challenges for the future of theological education. First, instead of fitting new technologies into old pedagogies, how are teaching and learning transformed by shifting needs of students who are "digital natives" or "digital immigrants" and/or distance learners? Second, instead of relying on note-takers and extended deadlines, what pedagogies virtually eliminate the need for "accommodations" for students with learning disabilities because courses are designed flexibly with resources and opportunities open to diverse learning styles and needs? Third, instead of engaging student diversity with the tools of the 1960s, what new teaching and learning strategies anticipate future student racial/ethnic demographics and interracial educational experiences? The Saint Paul faculty perceives that proleptic pedagogical strategies reflect the praxis and prophetic goals expressed in the seminary's mission and values, which challenge faculty to make theological education accessible and transformative for the next generations of seminarians.

The Proleptic Pedagogy project anticipated an impact on student learning because of pedagogical responsiveness to student learning needs. Stephen Brookfield proposes that critically responsive teaching is "guided by a strongly felt rationale but which in its methods and forms responds

7. Ibid., 8.
8. Ibid., 1.

creatively to the needs and concerns expressed by students."[9] By attending to how students experience learning and by acquiring new skills, methods, and approaches, the faculty anticipates more successful student learning because of clearer communication, more appropriate learning activities, and fitting pedagogical strategies. The faculty seeks to design courses and pedagogy open and accessible to multifaceted, diverse students, who express many learning styles and experiences and whose identities are racially and ethnically varied. The project models critically responsive teaching for students who serve the church as clergy and teachers.

The rationale for Proleptic Pedagogy is guided by analysis of theological education and student learning. *Educating Clergy*, a landmark study of theological education, names the diversity among seminarians that creates a complex learning environment for professional formation. Increasing numbers of women students, historically marginalized persons, older students, and religious traditions provide a valuable presence in the classroom, but also color the contemporary classroom with diverse expectations and experiences that create both opportunities and challenges in pedagogy.[10] *Educating Clergy* concludes that "increasing diversity of students in programs of clergy education has significantly challenged the ethos and mission of seminary education during the last forty years."[11] *The substance of the Saint Paul School of Theology proleptic pedagogy project was to anticipate the increasing and changing diversity of students to be expected in the next decade and to prepare faculty pedagogically and theologically to address teaching and learning in multidimensional ways.* The assumption of the project was that successful pedagogy requires expanding contextual awareness of and responsiveness to student diversity.[12]

The project anticipated three areas of increasing student diversity, which hints that the now familiar forms of diversity are in transition and require more nuanced pedagogical approaches. First is diversity created by differing access to and experience with digital technology. Second is diversity created by awareness of diverse learning styles, inclusive of learning styles associated with diagnosable "learning disabilities." Third is diversity generated by changing racial/ethnic demographics and increasing

---

9. Brookfield, *The Skillful Teacher*, 23.
10. Foster, Dahill, Goleman, and Tolentino, *Educating Clergy*, 54–55.
11. Ibid., 54.
12. Ibid., 57.

*Proleptic Pedagogy, Transition, and Teaching toward the Future*

populations of biracial and multiracial students. The following paragraphs elaborate the three categories of diversity.

Digital technologies, over the last two decades, have enhanced the experience of teaching and learning significantly, but not without particular challenges. As many forms of technology—ranging from email, the Internet, and presentation software to online library card catalogs, course management software, and classroom learning environments (such as Blackboard and Moodle)—enter theological education, pedagogies have stretched to respond to diverse student access and experience with digital learning tools. While some seminarians by generation, profession, or privilege are quite skilled with technology, others have limited access and ability related to available software, hardware, or Internet service providers; and some students still suffer lack of confidence with technology (even "technophobia"). Digital classroom resources pose at least two newer pedagogical challenges. One is the challenge to devise pedagogical strategies that simultaneously reach both *digital natives* and *digital immigrants*, Marc Prensky's terms for students who are "'native speakers' of the digital language of computers, video games and the Internet" and students who adopted new technologies later in life and, thus, "speak with an accent."[13] Prensky's most striking claim is that contemporary students "think and process information fundamentally differently" from previous generations of students.[14] The neuroplasticity of brains is such that organization and neural processing literally adapt physically to the digital context.[15] Typically a seminary faculty, made up of digital immigrants, must teach a student body of both digital immigrants and digital natives.[16] The second pedagogical challenge arises from increasing demand to provide simultaneous instruction at diverse learning sites. Online distance learning and videoconferencing create a new classroom climate that challenges faculty to create pedagogies that build community in a virtual world or among residential and distance learners. Delivery of learning resources, provision of individualized support, and stimulation of course engagement require new teaching and learning strategies.

Diverse learning experiences, styles, and abilities are not unique or new in theological education. Seminarians, for example, are frequently

13. Prensky, "Digital Natives and Digital Immigrants," 1–2.
14. Ibid., 1.
15. Prensky, "Do They Really *Think* Differently?" 1.
16. Prensky, "Digital Natives and Digital Immigrants," 2. My statement is a paraphrase of Prensky's point with an application to the seminary context.

students in vocational or educational transition into theological education from a college education or a first or second career, while very few enter seminary with preseminary or religion majors. The educational literature on learning styles and multiple intelligences, as well as generational learning experiences, has assisted seminary faculty in addressing the professional formation of students for ministry. Different educational backgrounds and abilities typically characterize the seminary classroom. In addition, increasing attention to "learning disabilities" has generated diagnostic tools, specialized learning strategies, and more hospitable policies and practices for inclusive learning environments. The first pedagogical challenge for seminary faculty is to remain current in the literature on changing and diverse learning styles. The second pedagogical challenge is to understand how to respond to both successful and weak students who are affected by learning disabilities in order to enhance the learning experience and to offer appropriate professional formation.

*Educating Clergy* identifies an increase in historically marginalized seminary students, largely as a consequence of the civil rights movement.[17] What may be typical of most seminaries, including Saint Paul School of Theology, is that our historical engagement with racial and ethnic minority students is focused on the Black-white racial divide. Our work with racism both in the content and context of theological education is not finished, and clergy education must continue to struggle with the historical enslavement of and discrimination toward African Americans that continue to affect seminary life and work. At the same time, new challenges and opportunities are arising with current and next generations of seminary students. The first pedagogical challenge must address the educational backgrounds of students who learned in integrated rather than segregated classrooms. Such students bring diverse encounters and experiences as part of their interpretation of race. The second pedagogical challenge is that increasingly our students are aware of and form identity as biracial or multiracial persons. The third challenge and opportunity concerns census data about increasing Hispanic populations in the U.S. While historically marginalized persons have long been part of the seminary ethos, the next decade promises a new racial and ethnic climate requiring a responsive awareness in pedagogy.

The approach of the Proleptic Pedagogy project included three key components to support faculty development. First, *Educating Clergy* encourages making conversations on teaching a community practice and

---

17. Foster Dahill, Goleman, and Tolentino, *Educating Clergy*, 55.

claims that "sustained conversations on teaching may be one of the most effective ways for seminary educators to strengthen their effectiveness as teachers."[18] The three-year project addressed the nuances of diversity by sustained conversations among faculty, building on and enhancing the habit of regular faculty reflection on teaching. Second, Stephen D. Brookfield (in *The Skillful Teacher*) writes, "One of the best ways you can gain insight into the experience of learning is to study your own learning."[19] The project borrowed from Brookfield the principle that "participation in formal educational activities provides a rich source of insights regarding how it feels to be a learner."[20] The three-year project included faculty language and technology instruction, which assisted in recalling the vulnerability of learning and providing new pedagogical skills. Third, Mary Hess claims that one concern in theological education is the contradiction of "Christian convictions and pedagogy."[21] The Proleptic Pedagogy project required faculty not just to engage in pedagogical conversation, but also to include theological reflection on identity and mission—developing a "theology of pedagogy" fitting Saint Paul School of Theology. Because the seminary's mission is the education of leaders for the church, the faculty anticipated that the Proleptic Pedagogy project would not only enhance teaching seminarians, but also would serve the church by anticipating the needs of the next generation of congregations.[22]

After three years of reading relevant literature, studying Spanish, attending workshops, revising courses, and developing projects, the faculty sustained our conversations about pedagogy in developing this collection of essays. The essays demonstrate that the faculty interprets the Saint Paul mission, theological education, theology, and pedagogy in diverse ways. Not to be interpreted as inconsistency, our diverse pedagogical approaches are our strength as we each contribute different teaching gifts and learning opportunities to the professional formation of our students. The intention of this book is to invite others into the conversation about the future of pedagogy, so that their unique proposals might emerge alongside ours.

---

18. Ibid., 369.
19. Brookfield, *Skillful Teacher*, 37.
20. Ibid.
21. Mary Hess, "What Difference Does It Make?" 88.
22. See, for example, Jewell, "What Does All *This* Mean for the Church?"

2

# Proleptic Pedagogy, Pluralism, and Pedagogical Agility

NANCY R. HOWELL

## Telling a Classroom Story

A SYLLABUS IS TWO-DIMENSIONAL, BUT a classroom is dynamic, organic, and multidimensional. Please understand that a syllabus is critical in mapping the shape of the course and communicating instructional design to students and colleagues, but when the syllabus meets the actual classroom setting and classroom community, the course on paper meets the living teaching–learning environment. How the course, envisioned in the syllabus, emerges during the academic term is largely determined by the pedagogical gifts, tools, and strategies of the instructor. Resembling a musical score, the syllabus is interpreted by a pedagogical artist who either brings the music to life or sadly diminishes its aesthetic. The musical metaphor must remember, however, that the syllabus as score is not prepared for or performed by a soloist, but is an ensemble piece. The ensemble is composed of students who bring diverse attitudes, skills, perspectives, and experiences to the music—and with each new semester, even the same course is expressed differently measure by measure.

The Advanced Praxis Seminar at Saint Paul School of Theology attracts diverse ensembles of students each semester, and the section taught by F. Douglas Powe and me, which focuses on "Theology in Black and

White," often attracts students interested in issues of race and theology, or students wishing to reconnect with the instructors because of a previous course, or students who find our course to be conveniently scheduled, or students who have heard about the course from other students. Regardless of their diverse reasons for selecting the course, all students have in common that they are nearing the end of their Master of Divinity program and are required to complete two Advanced Praxis Seminars, where they are asked to demonstrate the ability to integrate theory, theology, and practice.

Dr. Powe and I have taught the course several times since 2007, and each semester is memorable because of what students have taught us about course design, process, and pedagogy. In 2007, the course enrollment was small because of the new APS course requirement, and the all-female enrollment included African American and white women, as well as an African American female teaching assistant (a recent MDiv graduate with pastoral experience). In the next few years, the course settled into enrollments of twenty-five or more students, and the diversity of students multiplied exponentially. Denominational, theological, ethnic, class, gender, age, geographical, and unspoken differences created unique classroom textures. Simultaneously Saint Paul School of Theology became much more sophisticated in response to documented learning disabilities, even as we ventured into more advanced course technology with course management software and videoconferencing. Consequently some of the hidden differences—learning styles and disabilities, digital natives and digital immigrants—surfaced with greater intensity.

## Identifying the Pedagogical Challenges

Diversity in the classroom does not mean that we lose focus on the theme, objectives, and purpose of the course, but diversity challenges faculty to develop a pedagogical repertoire to enhance learning. The point of pedagogical agility is to reciprocate the challenge with students, so that we meet students at their points of academic strength, at least sometimes, and then provide other occasions for learning and practicing new skills that push students to achieve differently and build their learning repertoire, which seminary students can later apply to congregational contexts and responsibilities.

The challenge in theological education is not to catalog discrete elements of pluralism and create an additive mixture of educational techniques,

Proleptic Pedagogy

but to develop a proleptic pedagogy that anticipates both the short-term and long-term future of professional formation of students. The immediate needs of current students suggest that each semester must anticipate a progressive development of the learning community, as well as the individual and diverse students who contribute to the course. The more distant future of theological education requires a more holistic and adaptive approach to teaching and learning, which refuses to compartmentalize students even as we become more skilled in understanding the specific and contextual experiences that shape how they learn. If theological education is a formational and integrative process in the preparation of students for future ministries, then our educational approach should model anticipation. The challenges in theological education ask us to replace fear or avoidance of the unknown future with a climate of expectation and discovery. My suggestion is that *seminary faculty need pedagogical agility in order to enhance and enjoy the pluralistic learning environment often found in theological education, as well as to prepare ourselves proleptically for the future of professional formation.*

While classrooms and the future of theological education present many challenges, this chapter considers *teaching-learning technology, learning styles and disabilities, and racial and ethnic diversity.* Rather than imagine a content-less and vague future of theological education, the current classroom climate functions as a laboratory and microcosm for analysis of student learning needs and more specific issues, which are exemplified in the Advanced Praxis Seminar.

First, the Advanced Praxis Seminar experienced a progression of technological challenges in the seminary curriculum. In the early years, well-equipped classrooms encouraged faculty to use film, music, Internet resources, PowerPoint presentations, telephone interviews, and email to create stimulating learning communities and active learning experiences. When we used novels to elucidate what we meant by African American experience or the construction of whiteness, films sometimes helped students to engage the points better than written words alone. For example, a film clip from *The Color Purple* communicated the passion as well as the insight of the novel. Telephoning authors of assigned texts created living occasions to deepen, question, and contrast theological approaches. For example, a telephone (or Skype) conversation with Dwight Hopkins or Monica Coleman embodied ideas for students and gave students opportunities to interact with scholars who intrigued them. With the introduction of Moodle course management software, the learning curve for students and faculty escalated, but our novice use of Moodle enhanced communication. At least, we could post syllabi, resources, and assignments. In most recent years, Saint Paul School of Theology in Kansas City added a sister campus in Oklahoma City, and our approach to teaching and learning required use of videoconferencing to blend classrooms in two cities as we created access to full-time faculty.

Little imagination is needed to picture how changes in technology surface faculty and student differences. Even with a strong information technology staff, faculty and students learn by using Moodle or videoconference equipment, not just through instructional workshops on software. For some, exploring software and hardware is play and for others torture. Very soon frustrations and miscommunication result because of differences in familiarity with technology. Is the assigned paper late because a student could not access or use the technology, because the technology had a glitch, or because the student procrastinated? We can too easily assume that older seminarians are digitally challenged and younger students are digitally able, but the stereotypes did not hold as we noticed that access to high-speed Internet service, background with technology in previous education, and fundamental issues with reading or writing could impair student ability to participate well. Because faculty applied technology differently, students were sometimes confused about expectations. Such issues were apparent as early as the simple requests to submit papers by email and grew in proportion with each new digital teaching tool.

Learning styles and disabilities presented a second challenge. Many faculty members are familiar with literature on diverse learning styles and multiple intelligences, and we design courses and pedagogy to engage a diverse range of students. Few of us have training in the identification of or learning strategies to address learning disabilities, and rarely have we had explicit training in instruction for persons with learning disabilities. As our experience with the Advanced Praxis Seminar grew, the seminary's ability to accommodate students with learning disabilities increased. Earlier we had a vague sense of a documented diagnosed disability, and we provided extended deadlines or tutor support or peer note-taking. Now we can expect to receive 504 plans that inform us about specific accommodations that students may or must request. The diversity of learning needs is great among all students, but especially among those with conditions that make learning more difficult. Seminarians, especially those who completed secondary and university education some decades ago, often have not been equipped with skill-building or strategies for learning even though they are currently diagnosed with learning difficulties. Many students are reluctant to take advantage of the 504 plan accommodations or have problems overcoming the stigma of asking for help. While the issues were often hidden to faculty in our early years of teaching, better diagnosis, reporting, and institutional processes mean that we know how students struggle to learn, but we are not always clear about how to teach more effectively to students with learning disabilities. Consequently faculty responses are reactive—we create assignments, activities, and deadlines; student requests accommodations; then we respond to the request by giving more time or assistance. Even when instructors respond with great hospitality and sympathy, students have a sense of imposing.

Course design can complicate and derail student learning when learning disabilities necessitate accommodations in a structured framework. Our Advanced Praxis Seminar is designed with progressive assignments. We apprentice students in the process of identifying an issue and topic, researching a bibliography, developing a working thesis, writing a paper proposal, producing sequential paper drafts for faculty and peer review, and finally presenting the final written paper and oral discussion with the whole class. The tyranny of the sequence and deadlines, especially in conjunction with peer review, means that retroactive learning accommodations are challenging. A tension arises between providing accommodations and retaining the integrity of the learning sequence.

A third challenge is invited by the theme of the course, theology and race. Because the content of the course includes Black (liberation) theology, Womanist theology, and white theological writing on race, some challenges are obvious. White students express anger, frustration, denial, helplessness, solidarity, and regret. African American students experience anger, frustration, resentment, grief, hurt, identification, strength, and hope. Personal internal dynamics intersect with the social context of the student body, past experience with racial tensions or coexistence, and the intellectual project of critical thinking and analysis. Such challenges are perennial because U.S. history of Black–white racial struggle is the dominant paradigm of the course.

The new face of the racial and ethnic challenge is twofold. On one hand, students interested in the course are not necessarily white or African American. The enrolled students have ranged from Native American, Korean, and Latino/a to white and Black. One tendency is for students to resort to familiar personal, social, and academic territory, and the resulting challenge is to address the ability to listen patiently to the struggle of others before returning to one's own assumptions, struggles, and justice work. Sometimes convincing students that the personal benefit of deep understanding of another's worldview and experience eventually has value for ministry is a very difficult task. Deep listening and learning then suggest analytical, missional, and praxiological insight for other contexts, but the stimulation of ideas and feelings is strong and sometimes leads to self-referential focus that distorts or misses the wisdom of the African American context. For example, while Wesleyan thought may inform the discussion, students sometimes substitute abstract thinking about theology for engagement of Black critique of white theology. While Korean *han* generates rich and textured theology, developing an analogy between Black experience and Korean experience is contextually problematic. On the other hand, more and more students know themselves through much more complicated identities. Students and their families are more likely to identify as biracial or multiracial. When students are biracially Caucasian and African American, their relationship to course content is different than for students who self-identify as one or the other. Student ethnic or racial self-identification is entirely relevant to their motivations, attitudes, and expectations in the course. The pedagogical challenge is how to honor student identities and differences, as well as how to negotiate the shared stage of Civil Rights and Immigration issues in the United States.

No wonder that some instructors resort to their comfort zones when facing challenges of a seminary classroom. How tempting is a survival-of-the-fittest pedagogy that assumes good students survive and poor students perish in the rigorous classroom! Why not play to one's strengths as lecturer, PowerPoint presenter, or discussion leader and assume that good students—those really fit for ministry and leadership—will thrive and others will be eliminated from the ordination gene pool? Pedagogy of natural selection means that analysis of the classroom content, context, and community are unnecessary and that course and instructor evaluations are irrelevant and uninformative because of student biases about their performances in the course. In the end, the instructor may feel confident in his or her academic expertise, but angry and frustrated by some students who are characterized as lazy, distracted, unmotivated, ill-prepared, or stupid.

In contrast to pedagogy of natural selection, pedagogy of protection falls into the opposite trap of over-involvement with individual student learning. Theological education is a likely breeding ground for over-involved pedagogy because instructors are committed to service and inclusivity, but protection is equally problematic because the student can be disempowered or even made in the image of the instructor to the detriment of the student's growth and learning. Because I am more likely to fall into over-functioning in student learning, I have to monitor myself. For example, am I copyediting my student's writing or am I exposing students to the critique and instruction necessary to become a better writer? Am I inadvertently rewarding or requiring students to parrot my perspective or method or am I mentoring students in discovering and expressing their growing and developing theological perspectives? Protection and micromanagement generate student dependence on the instructor rather than eliciting engagement with learning and empowering students for life-long learning.

In my self-confessed struggle to move toward an empowering (and survivable) pedagogy, my pilgrimage began with issues of gender and race equity in the classroom and traversed to issues of learning disabilities. In the background loomed the specter of classroom technology—first as a pedagogical resource, but more recently as a defining difference in ways students learn. The nuance with which I perceive student diversity has grown exponentially, while my pedagogical expertise responds retroactively. Perhaps my slow responsiveness is related to the compartmented approach to addressing diversity in learning. What if instruction is not about teaching and gender equity, for example, but about more holistic, relational, and agile pedagogical skills?

Over a decade of research and workshops funded by the Wabash Center, I began to understand connections among learning styles and disabilities, race and student diversity, and digital natives and immigrants. The teaching–learning community will never be homogenous; my enrollment will never include cloned, environmentally identical students. However, the radical and increasingly heterogeneous classroom community is a true gift to teaching and learning, but not if we think that a metatheory of pedagogy addresses all facets of learning. When I observe student engagement, joy, and success in learning, the moment has usually been the result of more inductive and responsive intersections of pedagogical resources and opportunities, which enable students to find their unique ways into ideas, analyses, and applications.

## Engaging Pedagogical Literature

Reading *Diversity and Motivation: Culturally Responsive Teaching in College* by Margery B. Ginsberg and Raymond J. Wlodkowski convinced me that I am not alone in feeling stretched by diverse learning and pedagogical needs. The range and depth of student diversity affects university and theological education as academic eyes have learned to see beyond dominant culture. Ginsberg and Wlodkowski approach pedagogical questions with attention to the scope of learners in the classroom. They cite 2002 statistics showing that 73% of college students are non-traditional learners in the following senses: "delayed enrollment into postsecondary education, part-time attendance, financial independence, a full-time job, dependents other than a spouse or domestic partner, single parent, or nonstandard high school diploma."[1] In 2001, around 65% of adult students 25-years-old or older were women.[2]

Ginsberg and Wlodkowski embrace the view that learning contexts are never culturally neutral.[3] A central premise of their book is that the "influence of ethnicity, age, religion or spiritual orientation, socioeconomic status, sexual orientation, indigenous heritage, national origin, and gender require forms of pedagogical innovation that encompass and build on the diversities and similarities within classrooms and communities."[4] To their list we must surely add other categories of cultural difference, such as communities of persons with learning disabilities or diverse theological perspectives. The most daunting challenge in their statement is the requirement of *pedagogical innovation,* which implies that instructors must engage in both leave-taking (of normative pedagogical strategies) and constructing (of more culturally pluralistic, adaptive, and responsive pedagogies).

All instructors want students to be motivated about learning, but sometimes the tendency is to blame the student for lack of motivation rather than to reflect on classroom hospitality that welcomes and cultivates motivation. Ginsberg and Wlodkowski encourage making motivation the focus of pedagogical innovation. *Diversity and Motivation* emphasizes how important connecting with students' innate motivations is for innovative teaching and learning. Acknowledging that attention to and concern for student motivation is not new or unique, Ginsberg and Wlodkowski

---

1. Ginsberg and Wlodkowski, *Diversity and Motivation,* 5.
2. Ibid.
3. Ibid., 10.
4. Ibid., 27–28.

write, "Within our own teaching environments, we understand that students' concentration, imagination, effort and willingness to continue are powerfully influenced by how they feel about the setting they are in, the respect they receive from the people around them, and their ability to trust their own thinking and experiences."[5] Consequently creating hospitable learning environments and building a constructive, collaborative learning community are significant pedagogical concerns as we design and implement courses, but so is the process of knowing more than the content and topic of the course. We, as instructors, must know our students and assist students in self-awareness about how they learn, what authority figures have influenced what they know, how family traditions shape their values and interests, how they understand and practice their faith commitments, where they feel "romance" with ideas and questions, and what is valuable about their experiences as sources of knowing.

Transition to culturally responsive pedagogy (as a way to evoke student motivation) is not for the faint-hearted or culturally entrenched. First, culturally responsive teaching requires critical deconstruction of dominant culture as the explicit and implicit governor of the content, climate, and community. The point is not to erase dominant culture and traditions, but to place them in perspective with inclusive attention to diverse cultures that enter the classroom with students and with resources informing the course. For example, the teaching-learning environment must moderate the tendency for persons from dominant culture to monopolize class discussions or for faculty to establish classroom norms or practices that benefit persons from dominant culture to the detriment of persons from other diverse cultures. Instructors must address the predominant values in their disciplines as well as the culture-dependent character of illustrations or examples.[6] In the context of race and ethnicity, the transition to culturally pluralistic and responsive teaching means understanding the power of white privilege. In the context of deaf culture, teaching with regard to diversity requires breaking stereotypes and habits that privilege hearing persons. Instructors can easily confuse dominant academic paradigms with rigor, but our disciplines, at their best, espouse the principle that breadth of research and perspective ensure true rigor and critical thought. Privilege guards "unearned access to resources and social power, often because of

---

5. Ibid., 3.
6. Ibid., 18.

social group membership," and the pedagogical consequence is that bias and exclusion rob some students of motivation.[7]

Second, faculty must embrace the connection between student motivation and student cultural and experiential identities. Unfortunately the solution to motivation-deadening teaching is neither continuation of pedagogy and course design that cater to privilege nor creation of a one-size-fits-all replacement pedagogy. To access the places where students experience irrepressible motivation, faculty must become cultural interpreters rather than cultural scientists. Ginsberg and Wlodkowski explain this distinction by writing that cultural awareness is not reduction of culture to "a series of facts, physical elements, or exotic characteristics" to be learned and applied to classroom dynamics, but is an interpretive act that "takes into account that human beings are suspended in webs of significance that we create."[8] The pedagogical skill of interpretation is not vague or abstract, but concrete and explicit. Setting aside our own biases, we as faculty are called to devise cognitive, social, and interpersonal ways to know our students as well as we know the content of our courses.

Third, the teaching-learning environment must shift from extrinsic to intrinsic goals in order to maximize the learning potential of students. Ginsberg and Wlodkowski point out a distressing contrast between approaches to learning. With extrinsic goals, typically established by the instructor and her academic discipline, the rewards for achievement actually encourage students to seek "the least demanding and perfunctory way of ensuring the reward."[9] In spite of decades of educational literature documenting the inferiority of learning under the model of external rewards and extrinsic goals, the classroom continues to be the locus of "shallow conceptual understanding and less persistence in learning."[10] Ouch! By contrast, pedagogy that taps students' motivation and intrinsic goals not only stimulates the learning process, but also creates a more hospitable and successful learning environment for diverse students. *Diversity and Motivation* reminds readers that William Blake "believed that thought without affection separates love and wisdom," and similarly learning and motivation are inseparable. Learning is not a skill that must be imposed from the outside, and the tendency to impose learning is fatal to education. Hence,

7. Ibid., 12.
8. Ibid., 9.
9. Ibid., 26.
10. Ibid.

Ginsberg and Wlodkowski advance the view that intrinsic goals and motivation are critical for transformative, sustained learning. Motivation is the internal drive to devote one's energy toward a goal or purpose, and learning is the normal, active, and free process of "constructing meaning from information and experience."[11] Ginsberg and Wlodkowski entice instructors to enter the stream of lifelong learning when they write: "We constantly learn, and when we do, we are usually motivated to learn. We are directing our energy through the processes of attention, concentration, imagination, and passion, to name only a few, to make sense of our world."[12] Such is the attitude and inspiration that I aspire and long to create in the classroom.

Fourth, culturally responsive teaching (with the word *culture* understood in the broadest sense) is founded on the relationship of motivation and learning. Ginsberg and Wlodkowski encourage an orientation to multiculturalism in the classroom that empowers learners by attending to "equitable social power or cultural wealth within the context of classroom interactions."[13] Referring to a larger body of literature on multicultural sensitivity in the classroom, they advocate equitable teaching practices ("moral values, equitable hiring practices, and the content of curriculum"), which they term *culturally responsive* or *culturally relevant teaching*.[14] While some readers might take issue with the word *culturally,* I note that for the purposes of their discussion *culture* is defined as "the deeply learned confluence of language, values, beliefs, and behaviors that pervade every aspect of a person's life, and it is continually undergoing change."[15] In theological education, the classroom may be genuinely intercultural when we include Asian, African, and Latin American students or instructors, but the seminary classroom in also *intra*cultural when we take account of the full extent of diversity characterizing the demographics, histories, and social locations of our students. Students in the seminary bring a variety of meaning-making perspectives and diverse modes of learning to the classroom, which must be met by a teaching-learning environment. Ginsberg and Wlodkowski observe that the "larger the variety of relevant and effective practices teachers and learners know, the greater flexibility they have to support differences

11. Ibid., 27.
12. Ibid.
13. Ibid., 23.
14. Ibid.
15. Ibid., 9.

among themselves and the topics to be studied."[16] My argument is similar: seminary faculty need pedagogical agility in order to enhance and enjoy the pluralistic learning environment often found in theological education.

## Considering a Theology of Pedagogy

While technical pedagogical matters are critical, the heart of theological education is the theology of pedagogy that inspires building a learning community, evoking a creative learning climate, inviting an attitude of discovery, sharing a sense of wonder, and forming a life of discipleship. The theology behind my approach to pedagogy begins with God who evokes adventure, creativity, imagination, and possibility.

The God of adventure challenges pedagogy to take calculated risks for the sake of discovery, wonder, and creativity. The banking model of education (which is analyzed by Paulo Freire and bell hooks in contrast to much more liberative and transformative ends) is the antithesis of pedagogy consistent with the God of adventure. Filling minds with facts and ideas is not only deadening to the mind and spirit, but also ill-equips persons to be leaders and disciples in the church. Local congregations in their multifarious expressions of faith and community hunger for leaders formed by adventure, as persons follow the call of God shaped and informed by seminary education, but not limited by what they have learned. To be clear, theological education is critical in providing strong biblical, theological, historical, and practical models and traditions, but continuity with these paradigms is not simple repetition of the past. The inspiration of the tradition is the recapturing of wonder and adventure—the fearlessly faithful venture into the call of God that defies triviality and challenges leaders and disciples to meet the congregation and the world in fresh ways—as we are surrounded by the great cloud of witnesses whose living testimony en-courages and secures risks.

A relational concept of God is critical for my theology of pedagogy because community and relationship are the always dynamic, modestly predictable, often surprising generative contexts for creativity. Rather than solely emphasizing dependence on the instructor for intellectual and spiritual insight, the formational value of the learning community is enhanced by the intersection of instructional gifts, collaborative learning, historical liveliness, and divine imagination. Theological education forms persons for relational

16. Ibid., 42.

demands of ministry, which means that affirmation and breadth of community are core values. The community is ostensibly composed of faculty and students, but theological pedagogy expands the community to include figures as diverse as St. Augustine and John Cobb, as distant as Bishop Desmond Tutu and Gustavo Gutiérrez, and as subtle (or bold) as the holy and Christic presence of God. The depth and richness of community enhance theological imagination, which is necessary for responsively engaging ministry. Ministry is not formulaic, but is the creative and responsive work of continuous nurturing and building of an expansive faith community. A relational God embodies the community and inspires creativity within relationships as the unflagging source of possibility and novelty.

The God of risk and adventure advances the freedom and creativity of others by evoking potential rather than controlling events and ideas. The divine model suggests that instructors move beyond rigid classroom protocols to form interactive learning communities entertaining questions and possibilities. Not at all an abandonment of discipline, the classroom process becomes one of critical engagement privileging modes of thought, but informed by methodological and informational knowledge. Teaching and learning on this model meet the learning community and individual students at their particular places of inquiry, struggle, and curiosity by proposing questions, issues, ideas, purposes, and actions as heuristic devices to open minds to learning and hearts to God's call. The point is to create habits of reflection and life-long learning responsive to possibilities inspired by the call of God and open to the synergy of community. Theological education is enhanced by placing the evocative future imagined by God at the center of the classroom so that students and instructor alike approach theology not merely as prescriptive, but as a way of being, acting, and relating in the world.

The theology of pedagogy that guides my teaching aspires to an often unspoken mission statement. That mission is to evoke worshipful theological reflection open to the divine imagination and transformative for disciples committed to service in the church and world. The seminary classroom is at its best when the learning community coheres in God's empowerment of disciples whose spiritual depth and intellectual growth evolve as essential elements of professional formation for ministry. The spiritual and intellectual evolution of disciples is not merely an interior process of personal piety, but is also an exterior process with heightened insight about the needs of the church and society.

## Constructing a Pedagogical Proposal

Combining the insight of educational literature and the wisdom of theological perspective generates a challenging, but constructive motivational context for seminary faculties to re-imagine theological education at the curricular and classroom levels. The goal of pedagogical agility inspires reflection on the institutional, programmatic, and instructional work of theological education, but my constructive proposal begins in my classroom with an ever-shifting plurality of students. My primary focus for this essay is an experiment in how to anticipate student diversity at the stage of course design and syllabus development.

During the period of the Wabash grant, I developed an adaptable heuristic tool to help me remember details and analyze my course design and pedagogy. The device originally occurred to me as I reviewed my notes from a grant-supported workshop on learning styles and disabilities by Dr. Laura Hubbard, Associate Professor at Curry College in Quincy, Massachusetts, where her expertise includes working with students in the Program for Advanced Learning, which serves students with intellectual ability who are diagnosed with learning disabilities. The workshop for Saint Paul School of Theology faculty heightened our awareness of the diverse nature of learning disabilities and needs, but surely provided several clues about how our courses might be designed to create hospitable and motivating learning environments for diverse students.

The Learning Styles/Learning Disabilities Course Inventory (Table 1) is not a fixed or inflexible device, but a reminder and goad to keep students in focus as I design a course and prepare the syllabus. The first column of the table requires me to list specific elements of my course that address diverse student learning needs. The second column reminds me of the challenges that individual students may encounter in the process of learning, and the third column documents the corresponding styles and disabilities that characterize student learning. The table is adaptable to diverse courses and anticipated students, and the inventory grows and expands as I learn more about student modes of learning.[17] While I will not elaborate on every

---

17. While learning disabilities are relevant to all my courses, so are other considerations that require expansion of the table. For example, as I consider race/ethnicity or theological diversity in course design, I add a category in the table that encourages inclusion of authors who reflect the identity and motivations of students, as well as resources that challenge students to reflect on new questions, applications, and theological perspectives. The short-term goal is to engage students in theological reflection that seems

element of the inventory, I will highlight a few strategies for tapping student motivation in the course syllabus and introduction.

One feature of the inventory is inclusion of multiple strategies for conversations with students about how they learn, which is informative for course instructors, the individual students, and the whole learning community. The Class Participation Self-Evaluation (Figure 1) gives students an opportunity for self-assessment based on criteria related to preparation, participation, and attitude. Using the self-evaluation communicates course expectations, so that instructors and students begin the first week of class with a common understanding of what class participation means. In terms of communication about learning, the most important feature of the class participation form is that discussion of expectations permits conversation with students about how class participation is more than attendance and oral discussion, which affirms that diverse student bring multiple ways of being true participants in a course. When I work most effectively with the self-evaluation, I plan a careful discussion on the first day of class that probes what modes of participation are most comfortable for students.

A second way to invite discussion of student learning is review of the learning disability statement and related statements in the syllabus about student and instructor responsibilities in the course. At Saint Paul School of Theology, a good disability statement indicates that the seminary has resources to assess student learning disabilities, as well as a system for development of a 504 Plan for students with documented disabilities. I also include a statement reviewing student responsibilities specified in the handbook (such as attendance and academic honesty) with a complementary statement about instructor responsibilities (which I adapted from a similar statement used by Beth Kraig, Professor of History at Pacific Lutheran University):

> Our job is to teach with integrity the scholarship representative of our fields, to see that students learn as much as possible, and to create a comfortable environment for learning. These goals cannot be accomplished without genuine attention to the unique strengths, experiences, and expectations that both the professors and students bring to the classroom. Our goal is to provide encouragement and support for your learning. Sometimes flexible procedures and learning options are necessary to facilitate the

---

relevant to them, but then to provide an environment that facilitates growth and more advanced articulation of their theological voices. Ginsberg and Wlodkowski provide the pedagogical rationale.

kind of teaching and learning that should occur. We are anxious to hear what energizes you, what disappoints you, where you disagree, and what helps you to learn. PLEASE SEE US IF YOU HAVE QUESTIONS, CONCERNS, OR SPECIFIC NEEDS.

By emphasizing our dual interest in quality of scholarship and centrality of learning, Dr. Powe and I hope to indicate our attitude and priorities in the syllabus as we establish the learning climate. As they review the syllabus with the instructors, students become aware that expectations are specific and rigorous, but not without flexibility, because learning and professional formation are the purpose of theological education and multiple modes of learning may be necessary to achieve formational goals.

The quest to discover how students learn continues during the course in multifunctioning forms of discussion. Discussions in the course take many forms ranging from plenary to small group discussion, as well as face-to-face and online discussions. A variety of discussion formats enables students (digital natives as well as digital immigrants) to function in both comfortable and challenging opportunities for engaging course material. Because our course uses videoconferencing to link the Kansas City and Oklahoma City campuses, the success of the course requires blended and integrated usage of technology to manage class discussion and build the learning community. Each discussion must be planned and facilitated with intentionality by the instructors and students as we balance attention to multiple voices in two locations, sometimes using Skype to interview a scholar from a third location or focusing on a video clip or PowerPoint presentation simultaneously.

While the complexity of class discussion under these circumstances may sound overwhelming, the flexibility and variety are stimulating for learning and are a product of blending face-to-face, videoconferencing, and online modes of discussion not confined by a single geographical location and time period. Online discussions often achieve a depth impossible under limited time constraints, while they advance the face-to-face discussions that occur later—especially when the instructors use the online discussions to discover which ideas and methods are most difficult for or accessible to students. Synchronous and asynchronous online discussions enable peer or plenary groups to interact with instructors and course materials beyond the classroom and even on snow-cancelled class days. However, simply having the software, hardware, and space for discussion is not a guarantee of learning because the learning community must be supported by high quality questions and goads for discussion. For discussions to be effective, they must be relevant and important to students, and sources such as *Discussion as a Way of Teaching: Tools and Techniques for Democratic Classrooms* by Stephen D. Brookfield and Stephen Preskill are essential for equipping faculty to function as discussion leaders. Carefully crafted discussions create an inclusive collaborative space for students, who test their understanding and deepen their analysis of reading and resources or who engage each other in peer review of written assignments. In some courses, students with learning disabilities have indicated that online discussions resulted in ability to engage reading assignments more effectively because the discussion points function as reading guides, the questions have diverse levels of difficulty, the conversation with other students generates more confidence in understanding materials, the discussion includes both relevant interpretation and application, and required participation fosters accountability. Well-planned and organized discussions (in conjunction with clear class plans and transitions) assist students pedagogically and methodologically in theological education because we are not simply teaching ideas; we are teaching and modeling how to think theologically. When faculty develop discussions responsive to student learning styles, then each week of the course progressively engages the plurality and dynamics of the learning community.

Another way to mentor students in professional formation is to design assignments that are staged and developing over the course of the semester. The centerpiece of the Advanced Praxis Seminar that Dr. Powe and I teach is a twenty-page paper integrating theology and ministry, but a number of students have undeveloped skills in writing more complex, sustained arguments. In order to avoid papers that are products of poor research and planning or all-night writing sessions on the due date, we have developed a series of assignments that model how to undertake a rigorous theological research project with good time-management skills. The stages include brainstorming appropriate topics, writing a proposal (with a working thesis statement, research question, project description, and bibliography), rough drafts, peer review of other students' papers, and oral presentation of the final paper followed by peer response and questions from the class. Each stage of work permits the instructors to work with students to refine a project that holds meaning for the individual student. Interaction with students can entail routine work with library research or grammar, but more often means placing ourselves in the theological struggles of the students who are trying to find their theological voices in dialogue with Black and Womanist theology as they work to imagine how theological reflection can make a difference in congregational settings.

Because the projects are unique to each student, the assignments depend on student motivation. Individualized attention to student learning styles, experiences, theological perspectives, and ministry settings evokes the issues and concerns that are part of each student's professional formation. The pedagogical strategy is to maximize the relevance of the assignment to the students and their congregational or other ministry settings. When we are present to students and listen to their ministry experiences and theological questions, we become midwives in their processes of reflection and problem solving. Particularity and relevance are essential elements in the evocation of meaning-making, motivation, and learning. Student particularity is not a distraction from the course content, the writing assignments, or class discussions, but is the key to evoking love of worshipful theological reflection that sustains the life of ministry.

When course design is not restrictive of pedagogical flexibility, then the instructor can orchestrate movements in the classroom that motivate and facilitate learning that meets students in their particularity. For example, the previous online discussion signals what might need to occur in the next face-to-face discussion. Instructors might discover in the face-to-face discussion that the planned presentation on one concept needs to be replaced immediately by a more pressing conceptual challenge that prevents students from moving forward, or student questions might suggest that the energy of the classroom requires adjustment of activities or content. Another example is construction of assignments that encourage a range of imaginative thinking rather than limiting topics and research. Students sometimes select a course because of interest in the course description, and they imagine what they hope to learn and experience in the course. Rather than restricting all assignments to the same sources and topics, course design can be open to student interest and expectations by offering options in assignments, by requiring students to design projects of their own, or by creating student/faculty collaborations for research purposes. With such assignments, the instructor's pedagogical flexibility is expressed in the process of mentoring students in developing a research question, designing a research strategy, synthesizing a range of information, and devising a relevant application to ministry. Pedagogical flexibility is hospitable to student motivation and diversity.

Proleptic Pedagogy

Course design and the syllabus are the critical beginning for pedagogical flexibility in the classroom. Course expectations create the climate for diverse pedagogical movements and responses to student learning needs in the moment of instruction. The instructor interprets student motivation and discovery as a practice of pedagogical agility, but also anticipates the resources, information, and activities that must be prepared, discarded, reorganized, and improvised to respond to the tempo of the teaching-learning moment. *Seminary instruction needs pedagogical agility in order to enhance and enjoy the pluralistic learning environment often found in theological education, as well as to prepare ourselves proleptically for the future of professional formation.* Pedagogical flexibility is part of the craft of teaching that prioritizes student motivation and diversity.

Saint Paul School of Theology
MIN430 APS: Theology in Black and White
Spring 2009

Learning Styles/Learning Disabilities Pedagogy Inventory

| Activity or Strategy in MIN430 | Need Addressed | | Learning Style or Disability |
|---|---|---|---|
| Disability statement in syllabus | Diagnosis, documentation, and accommodation | | All disabilities (learning, developmental, intellectual, emotional, physical) |
| Daily course organizer (aka advanced organizer or class plan) | Problems with concentration (focus) and distractions—student language processing | | LD/ADHD |
| Name shifts in modality and transitions as you teach | Anxiety about transitions | | LD/ADHD (cannot shift styles/sets) |
| Literature (novels, poetry)→ plot, language, feeling, creativity (metaphor) | Left brain<br>Parts to whole<br>Analytical<br>Linear<br>Language | Right brain<br>Whole to parts<br>Gestalt<br>Creative<br>Emotional | Left and right brain tendencies |
| Talk to students about how they learn | Self-awareness and instructor awareness | | All styles and disabilities |

| | | |
|---|---|---|
| Guiding questions for reading<br>No tests | Problem with short term memory and long term memory<br>Need extended test time and reading time | LD/ADHD |
| Clear time management guide with stages for completion of larger assignments | Time management (especially when emotion hijacks learning)<br>Anxiety and other mental health issues are frequently comorbid with LD/ADHD, so these students are at risk at any point in the learning process for their emotions to hijack their brains. Students are vulnerable to feeling overwhelmed. | ADHD |
| Introduce papers and assignments with templates<br>Break up larger assignments<br>Allow extra time (through scheduling stages of completion)<br>Use intermediate deadlines<br>Use writing support (tutors and/or editing software) | Problems<br>In expressing and receiving language<br>In reading, spelling, writing, listening, and speaking<br>In translating thought into language and language into thought | Dyslexia |
| Don't use small groups all the time<br>Use Moodle course management software to develop threaded discussions effectively | Difficulty reading environmental cues<br>Difficulty reading people and relationships<br>Difficulty with perception such as spatial relationships<br>High intelligence and functioning frequently (just as people with LD/ADHD are frequently highly intelligent) | Nonverbal LD |
| Course organizer<br>Varied activities | Inattentive and/or hyperactive behavior | ADHD |

Table 2.1. The table was developed in collaboration with my teaching partner F. Douglas Powe, but is largely a result of information gathered in a workshop by Dr. Laura Hubbard of Curry College in Quincy, Massachusetts. Dr. Hubbard's recent suggestions refined the details about learning needs, styles, and disabilities.

Class Participation Self-Evaluation Work Sheet  Nancy R. Howell
Saint Paul School of Theology  F. Douglas Powe, Jr.
Fall 2011

Name: _____ Course: APS 430 Advanced Praxis Seminar

Circle the number that best describes your class participation in each category if 1 is excellent, 2 is very good, 3 is average, 4 is satisfactory, and 5 is poor.

## Preparation

| | |
|---|---|
| I conscientiously attempted all reading assignments. | 1 2 3 4 5 |
| I reflected seriously on reading assignments. | 1 2 3 4 5 |
| I worked to bring depth to comments and questions by preparing more than superficially for class. | 1 2 3 4 5 |
| I prepared written and online assignments on time and when they syllabus or my self-assigned deadlines required them. | 1 2 3 4 5 |
| I checked spelling, grammar, quotations, and footnotes/endnotes before submitting papers. | 1 2 3 4 5 |
| I posted papers on Moodle by the deadlines for discussion. | 1 2 3 4 5 |

## Class

| | |
|---|---|
| I attended class weekly. | 1 2 3 4 5 |
| I always attended class on time. | 1 2 3 4 5 |
| I contributed to class discussions. | 1 2 3 4 5 |
| When I talked in class, I remained focused on the topic of class discussion. | 1 2 3 4 5 |
| I listened respectfully to comments and questions raised by other students. | 1 2 3 4 5 |
| I brought my questions to class or to the professor. | 1 2 3 4 5 |
| I expressed disagreement constructively. | 1 2 3 4 5 |
| I shared my responsibilities for successful class discussions. | 1 2 3 4 5 |
| I supported other students efforts in class discussions or assignments. | 1 2 3 4 5 |
| I contributed to Moodle discussions and commented constructively on other students work. | 1 2 3 4 5 |
| I prepared for and contributed to peer discussion of student presentations. | 1 2 3 4 5 |

## Attitude

| | |
|---|---|
| I remained involved and engaged in the course. | 1 2 3 4 5 |
| I was constructive in relationships with others. | 1 2 3 4 5 |
| I put extra effort into the courseÑsuch as study groups/partners, library research, recommended or supplemental reading. | 1 2 3 4 5 |
| I contributed my share of the work in collaborative writing or projects. | 1 2 3 4 5 |
| I made appointments with a professor when I needed assistance or wanted to discuss the course. | 1 2 3 4 5 |
| I took responsibility for my learning. | 1 2 3 4 5 |
| My understanding of theology (especially theology as a way of life) has grown. | 1 2 3 4 5 |
| My understanding of ministry has grown through integrative thinking and practices of justice. | 1 2 3 4 5 |

I assign myself the following letter grade: _____
(Enter A, A-, B+, B, B-, C+, C, C-, D, or F in the blank.)

Please submit any additional reflection on class participation that should affect your grade in writing on the back of this page. This work sheet is intended to assist you in thinking about the quality of your class participation. Any interpretations, additions, or connections of criteria should be included in your additional reflections.

Figure 1. The Class Participation Self-Evaluation document has multiple purposes: (1) communication of class participation expectations, (2) discussion of student learning styles and motivations, (3) self-assessment by students of their course performance.

3

# From Objectifying to Contemplating the Other
*An Incarnational Approach
to Pedagogy in Theological Education*

ROBERT MARTIN

## Telling a Classroom Story

IN 2007 I TAUGHT the introductory seminar in our school's new DMin program in the beautiful and hospitable nation of South Korea. The course was titled, "Congregational Studies," which is an assortment of sociologically informed tools for understanding one's context more fully. Perhaps I should have taken the subject matter more seriously myself, for I was wholly unprepared for the Korean students' antipathy toward studying their congregations and communities. Only after my efforts at teaching failed miserably did I discover that studying a congregation or the surrounding community made little sense to these students. Given the alarming indications of decline among mainline Protestants in Korea, they understood their primary responsibility to do whatever worked in their context to grow their pastoral charge. Therefore, methods for investigating the identity and purpose of a congregation seemed irrelevant and distracting from their prime directive: *make disciples for Jesus Christ*.

Proleptic Pedagogy

On the last day of the course, as an act of desperation, I pulled out an exercise that I hoped they would at least enjoy discussing. It was a relatively simple but highly suggestive spiritual types survey by Dr. Corine Ware that distinguishes between four types of spiritual sense-making—"cognitive, emotional, kinesthetic, and mystical."[1] The goal of the survey is to surface which type of spiritual sense-making each individual naturally prefers more than the other types. After silently filling out the survey, the students turned to one another and started discussing the results. Soon, the room vibrated with their enthusiastic conversation. Apparently, the concept of a spiritual typology was completely new to them and the more they talked about it, the more puzzles in their own spiritual lives the typology seemed to resolve. It helped to explain why one person loves to pray contemplatively while others dislike it; why for some of the students, music is more spiritually enriching than sermons; why hands-on mission fulfills some people and not others. They energetically compared their spiritual preferences with each other, and in the comparison were better able to name many of the similarities and distinctions among them.

After I convened the small groups into a general discussion, a quiet and retiring voice rose from the back of the room, and wondered aloud whether there might be as much diversity of spirituality among their congregants as was evident among the gathered pastoral leaders. A wave of enthusiastic consensus resonated among the students, and my heart beat a little faster. The voice continued, prompted by the Spirit no doubt, to ask what implications for pastoral leadership that spiritual diversity in the congregation might suggest. At that moment the collective consciousness in the room shifted dramatically as they began to identify important distinctions. I was elated as questions about their calling to ministry and the normal patterns of congregational life surfaced. For example, many in the class mused about their own spirituality and whether the standard congregational practices, to which they were so dedicated, were spiritually enriching. Some complained that they felt alone and spiritually depleted in ministry. Others wondered how they might discover which congregational practices were spiritually fulfilling for the congregants and would help them really grow in discipleship. I wasn't sure whether I should be happy or sad that in the final hour of the course students began to be curious about their own spirituality and the spirituality of their congregants.

1. Ware, *Discover Your Spiritual Type*.

Only a couple years later, during the students' work on their DMin praxis theses, did the significance of that educational moment become apparent. It initiated a process whereby the students refocused their attention to their own spiritual identity and vitality and then reconceived their ministerial vocation and profession in light of it. Reprioritizing their own spirituality and discipleship over professionalism, and reinforcing that prioritization repeatedly through the DMin curriculum changed the way most of the students related to their congregations. Rather than seeing congregants primarily as objects of their ministerial action, most of the students discovered a more communal—and life-giving—approach to church life and leadership.

## Identifying the Pedagogical Challenges

It is an overstated truism that the world is becoming more connected and that greater diversity is emerging even in the most remote places. Not only cosmopolitan cities, but also seemingly isolated rural areas and toney suburbs are increasingly populated with people who look, act, believe, and love differently. Congregations need their clergy to help them interpret and engage the pluralism theologically and spiritually in a manner consistent with the gospel. For this reason, theological educators need to examine the educational environment and processes as to whether they help or hinder students' preparation for ministry in communities of increasing 'otherness.' This concern and two themes associated with the Wabash grant on proleptic pedagogy at Saint Paul School of Theology—racial/ethnic diversity and learning styles—inform this chapter.

In my experience, I have found that intercultural education is increasingly subverted by a growing anxiety about the institutional viability of Christian congregations. Religious authorities tend to associate Christian leadership with the strategies and techniques of institutional growth under the moniker of "making others into disciples of Jesus Christ." But if the operative understanding of ministry is primarily to "make" others into something they are not, then the default relation of minister to "other" will likely be unilateral, objectivizing, and instrumentalistic. It took an excursion half-way around the world for me to become more aware of—and concerned about—the subtle instrumentalization of ministry that objectifies the other, both within and beyond faith communities.

Proleptic Pedagogy

On the long trip back to the United States, I reflected on my experience in that course, and I wondered why the Korean students would be initially uninterested and reactionary against investigating their congregations and communities. I was curious about their rather intentional lack of curiosity. Above all, I was drawn to an interesting contradiction in their thinking about ministry and leadership. Most of the students were in their 30s and were associate pastors chafing under the patriarchal authoritarianism of the senior pastors. Their criticism of this conventional understanding of church leadership was informed, sharp, and insightful. However, almost without exception, when describing the nature and practice of church leadership in class, a nicer version of patriarchal and authoritarian leadership emerged as their default position. They seemed to resort to the socially dominant convention even though they called for something radically different.

As I mulled over this dichotomy, I recalled the illuminating work by Rabbi Edwin Friedman, who brought family systems theory to bear upon the trenchant issues facing religious institutions and their leadership.[2] He diagnosed the current dysfunction in society and its institutions as largely due to lack of competent and visionary leadership. He believed that leadership was systematically eroded by a pervasive climate of anxiety in modern societies. Reflecting back upon my visit in Korea, Friedman's diagnosis rang true. From my first introduction to the country, and especially among the Methodists there, the theme of mainline Protestant decline was constant. It seemed that everyone was urgently seeking the Holy Grail that would reestablish their churches on an upward trajectory.

To understand this phenomenon more fully, I re-immersed myself in Friedman's analysis of "anxious systems" that were defined by the anxiety associated with the least healthy member and the instability of the system as it revolves around pathology rather than health.[3] When congregational systems are influenced by the persons who are most anxious and dependent, the entire system becomes dysfunctional as it revolves around the dysfunction of the lead members. Friedman pointed to a number of characteristics of anxious systems, as illustrated in family therapy, but two are most pertinent to our topic.[4] First, anxious systems generate a heightened

2. Friedman, *Failure of Nerve*.

3. Friedman's understanding of an anxious system is based on the systems theory Dr. Murray Bowen used to explain emotional dysfunction within families. Dr. Friedman called these relational fields "anxious systems" and applied this family systems theory to congregations. See ibid., 10.

4. Friedman, ibid., 75–76.

level of reactivity that undermines the ways that people interact and think together.[5] Normally easy-going and relaxed relations become more reactive and brittle and conflicts flare up. Second, anxiety is discomforting and disrupting to established patterns, and people try to avoid or suppress these types of situations. If they can't avoid them, they try to fix them quickly and superficially. Rather than seek what Ronald Heifetz called "adaptive change" that addresses underlying causes, anxious systems prefer technical solutions which never sufficiently address the trenchant dynamics that foster the anxiety in the first place. Deep and penetrating analyses of the problematic situation are supplanted by the insatiable need for quick-fixes.[6] Within a charged emotional atmosphere, inquisitive, careful, and contemplative deliberation between differing perspectives is hard to come by and out-of-the-box solutions are discounted out of hand as people contract and conserve even as they say they want to progress. Consequently, conventional thinking about problems and solutions reigns supreme.[7]

In the Korean context, our students desperately wanted to change denominational decline to growth, but they seemed to be reverting instead to the dominant conventions of congregational life and leadership. They were not, at first, keen to explore alternative models of church life. They defaulted to a model of leadership that they felt objectified both themselves and the congregants. When confronted with critically engaged and transcendently oriented theological education, their initial response was reactive and dismissive for it did not serve their pragmatic goals for church growth instrumentally. But when the educational focus was redirected from the congregation and their professional identity to a more spiritually personal and profound dimension, the process of self-exploration generated a new openness to and curiosity about their profession, the congregation, and those with whom they are in ministry.

Returning to the United States, I reflected on my teaching experiences and the extent to which Friedman's diagnosis of social anxiety might help me understand how it subverts the spiritual nature and the training of ministerial leadership. Whether or not entire societies are becoming more anxious is a matter best left to others to work out, but it is all too apparent that American society is being culturally polarized by emotional reactivity that

---

5. Ibid., 13, 85.

6. Ibid., 106, 112.

7. Cf., Steinke, *Congregational Leadership in Anxious Times*; and Steinke, *How Your Church Family Works*.

denigrates social discourse and renders even the highest deliberative bodies in the land reactive and dysfunctional. Likewise, mainline denominations in the United States and in most developed countries are increasingly anxious about declining membership, resources, and social status, and their ability to substantively address trenchant issues is increasingly suspect. As demonstrated by the most recent United Methodist General Conference, failed efforts to address systemic and structural problems largely reinforce widespread skepticism and intensify anxiety that anything substantive can and will actually change at the denominational level. Many church officials have instead placed their hopes for transformation on leadership at the congregational level.

But a focus on the great leader is problematic as well. Within a culture of hero worship that "waits for superman"[8] to save it, many students, professors, religious officials, as well as people in the pews, believe that our only hope to reverse institutional decline lies in pastoral leaders who are problem-solving change agents. It is believed that the Church will only be saved by church leaders who effectively make disciples, cast visions, rally the troops, overcome obstacles, and organize communities to do what they otherwise wouldn't. From the early 1950s, scholars in business management studies defined leadership in terms of effectiveness, the capacity to accomplish tasks that further the interests of the group.[9] Surely, we can agree that leaders should be effective, but the larger questions—effective at *what*, effective *how*—can only be answered by reference to an underlying ideology or theology that supplies the worldview and standards by which to judge efficacy. Without that larger framework to guide action, we normally resort to what has worked in the past or what is working currently for most people, whether or not that action and its results are theologically warranted. I believe the profession of ministry has largely been captivated by just such a mindless pragmatism.

Pragmatic professionalism, however, is not without an ideology. On the contrary, the pragmatic professionalism of ministry has emerged within a much larger ideological framework that uncritically fuses Christianity and capitalism. In the interesting book, *Christianity Incorporated: How Big*

---

8. This phrase refers to the documentary on public education titled "Waiting for 'Superman,'" directed by Davis Guggenheim, 2010. It is an exacting portrayal of educational decline amidst seemingly intractable problems that can be reversed and redeemed only by a savior. The educational system appears to be incapable of constructively working on the problems, and so it seems that everyone is waiting for Superman to save them.

9. French and Raven, "The Bases of Social Power," 150–67.

*Business Is Buying the Church*, Budde and Brimlow argue that churches have been seduced by capitalism and its strategies, such that the relation between big business and the church resembles "institutional cross-dressing, in which churches and big corporations can't wait to run around in each other's clothes, each trying to pass for the other."[10] The conflation of Christianity and capitalism has gotten to the point, argues United Methodist Bishop Ken Carder, that "the most pervasive logic or vision for ministry today is shaped by the market and the values of consumerism rather than by the gospel of Jesus Christ."[11] If Bishop Carder is correct that Christian life and ministry is largely framed within capitalistic logic, and I believe he is, then we would expect church leadership, and especially the professional training of clergy, to be affected as well. This is exactly what we find. Seeking to reverse declining numbers of members and finances, denominations have incorporated managerial and bureaucratic methods of "normalizing" clergy education toward effective church (insert "institutional") growth, and that growth is most often measured according to objective and impersonal standards: how many members joined, how much the bottom line increased, etc. As ministerial leadership and training becomes increasingly quantified, it necessarily becomes increasingly instrumentalist and functionalist, which subsumes even the personhood of clergy to the roles and tasks that are most pragmatically useful to the institution.

When ministerial leadership and seminary education have professional success as their main goal, then the proper theological orientation of ministry will be overshadowed by the principles of professionalism. Professionalism shifts one's primary orientation away from theological faithfulness to worship lesser gods of institutional and programmatic development and success. When changing others and developing institutions becomes the primary, default purpose of church leadership, then the profession of ministry will likely be distorted in several ways:

a. Instrumentalist pragmatism: the pastoral vocation and identity is oriented more and more to solving problems and persuading people with whatever techniques work, regardless of theological/spiritual integrity. Leadership easily becomes preoccupied with problem-solving rather than mission, tasks rather than relationships, and the exercise of power *over* others rather than *with* others.

10. Budde and Brimlow, *Christianity Incorporated*, 7.
11. Carder, "Market and Mission."

b. Ministerial objectification of others: persons become the objects of the pastoral drive to make them into disciples of Jesus Christ rather than partners in a common Christian life. Programs and activities are devised *to* or *for* the people, and a great deal of energy is expended trying to persuade and cajole them to participate. It can easily become a self-reinforcing cycle as one's sense of reward and fulfillment in ministry is contingent upon whether one's efforts to change the other have been successful, and so one tries ever harder to change others in order to enjoy a sense of vocational satisfaction.

c. Objectification morphs into instrumentalism: When one is primarily concerned with institutional growth and one's own professional success, inevitably, people will be treated as means to those ends, not as intrinsically valuable in themselves. Rather than engaging the other with mutual regard with a posture of open hospitality as proposed by Kathleen Talvacchia,[12] an instrumentalist approach treats those within as well as those beyond the congregation as the objects of their well-intentioned designs.

d. The authentic spirituality of ministerial professionals suffers: when ministerial leadership is primarily understood as the exercise of changing and directing others to do things they otherwise wouldn't, then the professional energy of ministry is directed externally toward the people and programs that one is trying to direct and control. Ministry is mainly experienced as spiritually depleting as ministers expend their energy outward. They have to go elsewhere, other than the context of their ministry, to replenish their spiritual reserves. Of course, ministers need to distinguish themselves from their primary context of ministry. But when ministry becomes increasingly divorced from a mutual process of spiritual enrichment and renewal that involves clergy and laity, ministry more easily slips into a pragmatic professionalism that is categorically divorced from one's spiritual practice and well-being.

How might pragmatic professionalism be detrimental to theological education? The answer is rather straightforward: if ministry is characterized by pragmatic professionalism, and if theological education is oriented toward the professional training of ministry, then education itself will be inevitably influenced as well.

12. Talvacchia, *Critical Minds and Discerning Hearts*, especially chapter 2: "Listening and Understanding."

A recent teaching experience was particularly illuminating about the impact of pragmatic professionalism on theological education. I was asked by a colleague to take one of his classes while he was out of town. It was a systematics course on the doctrine of the Incarnation. My session with the students was to follow five classes of very rigorous academic material. Most of the students had been in class with me before, and my approach is explicitly incarnational, so I naturally planned to build on that foundation with advanced level material. To begin the class I asked them to define "incarnation." I thought this exercise would be a no-brainer, but to a person, each definition was abstract, vague, and simplistic. No one referred to or drew upon an authoritative resource. Inwardly, I was shocked and dismayed. But through a debriefing exercise, I tried to explore gently the students' thinking about why they were unable to define clearly the central term of the course.

The students readily acknowledged their conceptual fuzziness but were unable to identify reasons for it. When I brought up the topic of church leadership as one of the overarching goals of their education, most of the students described the chief responsibilities of ministry to include increasing attendance, raising funds, managing conflict, and growing the institution. They characterized their ministerial identity in terms of directing others and quick-fix problem-solving within their communities. The conversation then moved to reflecting on how pragmatic professionalism affected their learning.

One of the insights that surfaced in the discussion had to do with how they engage and store information. We found that they tend to filter education through two main categories: that which is useful day-to-day in ministry; that which is useful to pass courses. Only infrequently do the two meet. Because so much of their seminary education did not appear immediately relevant to the day-to-day concerns of their current ministries, students were not storing the information to use for future ministry when their personal and professional situation will most likely be very different. When they completed a course, for all intents and purposes, they left much of that material behind.

Within a narrowly professionalized pragmatism, it makes sense to divide theological education into esoteric, abstractions and immediately applicable knowledge. But of course, theological education is a rich ecology of knowledge and practice, some of which will be practicable in the short-term, but most of it is heuristically oriented toward the future in terms of personal and social transformation. In order to benefit as much as possible, students need to be able to access and draw creatively upon their education not only in the short-term but also for the long-haul and in diverse contexts.[13]

Convinced of my findings and with a sense of urgency, my first approach to the problem of pragmatic professionalism in theological education was rather dogmatic and strident. I diagnosed the situation *for* the students and prescribed and enforced remedial action for them to take, whether they wanted to or not. In many ways my action elicited equal and opposite reactions, for the students rightly felt my approach was somewhat demeaning and manipulative. That ill-considered, anxiety-ridden approach simply mirrored the problem of objectivizing others for the purpose of changing them. I was sent back to the drawing board. Rather than teach by default, I wondered what might be a more theologically informed and spiritually attuned response. To this purpose, we turn our attention to the literature on pedagogy of mindfulness and a theological framework for a pedagogy that might help students become more aware of and intentional about engaging reality deeply so that they learn more comprehensively and holistically.

## Engaging Pedagogical Literature

To reorient both teachers and students to a more robust *theological* pedagogy, we could talk about any number of strategies, but I want to introduce the practice of mindfulness as an incarnational approach that will mitigate the effects of objectivism and instrumentalism in theological education. Mindfulness is a term that is used in many religions, especially Buddhism, referring to a contemplative discipline of non-anxious, non-striving awareness. In Christianity, mindfulness is associated most with contemplative prayer such as centering prayer and *Lectio Divina*. The concept of attending gently and open-mindedly has also been a constant, if subordinated, theme in education. But now pedagogies that are self-described as contemplative or mindful are gaining greater prominence among educators, such as Wioleta Polinska, who are concerned with the formation of students who can engage our pluralistic society with less fear and prejudice and greater receptive awareness toward others.[14]

13. Talvacchia, "Integrative Educational Strategy," 139–45.
14. Polinska, "Engaging Religious Diversity," 159–67.

## Mindfulness in Educational Practice

Judith Simmer-Brown and Fran Grace define contemplative mindfulness as it applies to classroom environments: "conscious and gentle focusing of the mind on an object such as the breath or a phrase or sound, and the continuous return of attention back to that object again and again."[15] Mindfulness is a contemplative state of mind exercised more broadly: "the ability to remain present with this focus of attention, at first in a formal session of practice and eventually in varied and distracting environments that are more challenging."[16] The research of Ellen J. Langer, professor of psychology at Harvard University, has brought a more analytical concept of mindfulness to the fore in the sciences of consciousness and also in educational theory. She distinguishes mindfulness from mindlessness: allowing the distinctions and categories of the past to govern behavior and thinking regardless of the present situation. When we repeat patterns expecting different results then our thinking is mindless. On the other hand, mindfulness, as Langer understands it, draws "novel distinctions" to help us respond constructively to present circumstances.[17] That is, being mindful entails a movement of consciousness beyond received, conventional categories so that one has greater sensitivity to nuances, greater awareness of multiple perspectives that one might take, and openness to new information by which one engages a situation more adaptively.[18] Three practices are especially evocative of increasing mindfulness: sustained observation with attention to novelty and anomaly, intentionally exploring multiple options and possibilities, and the introduction of ambiguity and complexity so that one holds one's knowledge provisionally but with conviction.[19]

In both its contemplative and analytical modes, mindfulness is the practice of attending to reality more fully. It is an indispensable discipline for individual and collective discipleship to train the mind and body to remain present and focused as with a "deep, disciplined, nonjudgmental listening."[20] The purpose of mindfulness, as we are employing the term here, is to *awaken* in a non-anxious manner to the complexity, ambiguity,

---

15. Simmer-Brown and Grace, "Introduction," in *Meditation and the Classroom*, xxii.
16. Ibid.
17. Langer and Moldoveanu, "Construct of Mindfulness," 1.
18. Ibid., 1–3.
19. Ritchhart and Perkins, "Life in the Mindful Classroom," 31.
20. Coburn, "Convergence of Liberal Education and Contemplative Education," 5.

and depth of reality. "The goal of mindfulness practice is not to change our experience; rather it is to change our relationship to our experience."[21] That is to say, we already and always experience reality; the purpose of mindfulness is to become more aware, and as a result more responsive, to the particulars, depths, and dimensions of reality. This purpose is distinct from and more fundamental than (but not antithetical to) a pragmatic approach. If we prioritize mindfulness over pragmatism, then the two can be complementary because being more aware helps us act more critically and creatively, and thus more effectively.

### Mindfulness in Theological Education

When concerned with theological learning, in that the ultimate object of our learning is *theos* and of everything in relation to *theos*, being more aware of and dwelling within that ultimate dimension is absolutely crucial to our ability to lead and guide others into it as well. One of the consultants funded by our Wabash grant, Mary E. Hess, argues convincingly with her colleague Stephen D. Brookfield that the emphasis on formation is what makes theological education distinctive. Because religious knowledge has to do with how people engage the world in its depths, it should develop two types of capacities: "awakening and deepening of spiritual awareness" and the "human qualities of empathy, compassion, and love."[22] Calling our attention to the inescapably pluralistic context of religious life, theological pedagogy should be understood fundamentally therefore as "a matter of spirit, of understanding and appreciating the essential humanity and capacity for love that manifests itself in those of different faiths, races, cultures, and ideologies."[23] It is because of its existential and societal significance that Harvard professors Ron Ritchhart and David N. Perkins urge teachers to consider mindfulness as much more than instructional techniques but as a formative process that "permeates the lives of both teachers and students."[24]

Four principles about mindfulness guide our thinking. First, because mindfulness is employed across many religions and academic disciplines with different meanings, we will use the term mindfulness as the category that includes both contemplative and analytical awareness. J. Carmody

---

21. Polinska, "Pedagogy of Mindful Contemplation," 165.
22. Hess and Brookfield, "How Can We Teach Authentically?" 4.
23. Ibid.
24. Ritchhart and Perkins, "Life in the Mindful Classroom," 29.

describes it this way: "intentionally paying attention to present-moment experience (physical sensations, perceptions, affective states, thoughts and imagery) in a nonjudgmental way and thereby cultivating a stable and non-reactive awareness."[25] Second, because the resources upon which we are drawing use contemplation and meditation interchangeably, we will do the same. We will be most interested in disciplines that orient consciousness to the full reality of an object of some sort: to scripture, to art, or to the divine life of communion, as well as to depth dimensions within the most mundane activities.[26] Third, the relation between analysis and contemplation within mindfulness is asymmetrical with contemplation as more fundamental and analysis as secondary but essential. In this respect contemplation orients us to the existence in and upon which all other dimensions of life are sustained in their integrity. The fourth principle at work here is that of holism and comprehension: we should think of mindfulness, and its contemplative and analytical modes, in as holistic and comprehensive a manner as possible. Not only is it a religious/spiritual practice of the first order, but it is also a practice of training the mind in any discipline, regardless of whether one is religious or not.

Contemplative prayer is the practice of mindfulness in the form of a wordless prayer that challenges conventional understandings of prayer as primarily petitionary, thanksgiving, intercessory, etc. Rather than mostly talking *at* God, contemplative prayer is about resting in and listening for the Spirit whose communications are too deep for words. If theological education and church ministry are primarily a matter of participating more fully in the divine life so that it can be more fully manifest in and through us, then as Parker Palmer notes, we desperately need disciplines that will help us rest in and submit to that which is not of our own making.[27] Contemplation is a form of prayer that over time and with repetition challenges the dominance of the ego and reorients persons with openness to that which is not self-produced. It slowly transforms persons and communities through a humble receptivity to the holy Other. All other leadership skills, authority, and power are rightfully constituted only within such a transcendent and submissive orientation.

---

25. Carmody, "Evolving Conceptions of Mindfulness in Clinical Settings," 271.

26. This implies that we will not be referring to objectless awareness, which is sometimes called "mindfulness meditation"; cf. Mipham Rinpoche, "How to Do Mindfulness Meditation."

27. Palmer, *Courage to Teach*, 105.

Proleptic Pedagogy

Contemplation does not need to be cast in religious or spiritual terms. It can be understood as a secular discipline that creates distance between our personhood, or sense of self, and the thoughts and emotions of the ego. It should be said that the ego, whether individualistically or collectively conceived, is absolutely necessary to human functioning. The ego is the capacity to direct our lives and make things happen, and so we must have a healthy ego to live a healthy life. But the industrial, commercial, and academic systems of the Western world are built upon the supremacy of the ego. The pace, complexity, and productivity of contemporary societies demand that the ego function way beyond its healthy capacity, and literally we are driving ourselves insane.

The ego is not meant to dominate every other mental operation. Proper ego function demands that it be subordinate and submissive in two crucial respects: healthy ego function is completely dependent upon rest, namely, the quality of sleep. Without just a few days of sleep, persons begin hallucinating and quickly suffer mental breakdown. The second dependency of the ego is more subtle but just as vital. As defined by Sigmund Freud, the executive function of psyche, the ego, is tasked with maximizing pleasure and avoiding pain.[28] The more one's sense of "self" is narrowly construed and the more individualistic and hedonistic its aims, the more infantile and antisocial one's behavior will be. But as Heinz Kohut observed, when the sense of self expands and is more inclusive—especially of the "other"—the ego can function more altruistically and idealistically for the common good.[29] Contemplation disciplines the ego to submit to the self as it expands to include the truly other within the ultimate context of the holy Other.

In the practice of Christ-like leadership, contemplative awareness is vitally important, for it expands the self and subordinates the ego to the self. A brief example may illustrate: suppose a pastor is in her office and another woman barges in and verbally accosts the pastor. In that moment, the pastor's defenses are on high-alert, her heart races, and her ego instinctively presents two options: fight or flight. But neither option serves the ultimate *telos* of ministry: communion with God. The discipline of contemplation, sustained over time, distinguishes self from ego, and allows self to center itself non-anxiously in a more comprehensive reality which includes and

---

28. Freud, *Beyond the Pleasure Principle*.

29. Once a protégé of Sigmund Freud, Heinz Kohut reoriented psychoanalysis to a psychology of the "self" as the core of the psyche. See the initial theoretical development of his approach in Kohut, *The Analysis of the Self*, 1971.

permeates even the threatening congregant. The self is not swept up in the ego's thrashing, the mind's buzzing thoughts, or the heart's swirling emotions. Rather, the self is oriented to the Ground of its being and to the Spirit within the other person. To be contemplatively disciplined means that in the midst of a relational storm, the self can remain somewhat centered and calm, and attune herself to the depths within the congregant as well as to the Spirit who pervades the entire event. Thus grounded, ego obeys the self and finds strategies beyond fighting or fleeing in order to accomplish the higher purposes of the self. Such a *self-expanding centeredness* allows the leader to be more attentive to the Spirit's working and the hidden potential within situations, especially those that are most problematic.

## Considering a Theology of Pedagogy

The living font and ontological basis of theology—and thus theological education—is ultimately the relation of Creator and creation, for it is only in that relation that we are able to know of the Creator and of ourselves and the entire universe as related to the One Creator. In short, ontology is the only true source of epistemology and education. So theological education needs a theology that helps us clarify that ultimate relation, for everything that is said afterward about the church and its leadership should be derived from the Creator/creation relation and should lead us into participating in it more fully. The relation of God and the universe has found innumerable expressions throughout history, but two models are enough for a fruitful comparison: Monarchy and Incarnation.

### *A Monarchical Model of God*

In the book, *Models of God*, theologian Sallie McFague characterizes the monarchical concept of God ruling over his kingdom of heaven and earth as the dominant model of God in the West.[30] Echoing Gordon D. Kaufman, McFague argues that the monarchical model cultivates "a pattern of 'asymmetrical dualism' between God and the world, in which God and the world

---

30. It should be noted that the discussion about the monarchical model of Creator reigning over the creation is categorically distinct from the Catholic and Orthodox doctrine of the Monarchy of the Father within the Triune God. This is not the place to discuss that intra-Trinitarian structure, but simply to note the fact that we are addressing the relation of Creator and creation.

are only distantly related and all power, either as domination or benevolence, is on God's side. It supports conceiving of God as a being who exists somewhere apart from the world and rules it externally either directly through divine intervention or indirectly through controlling the wills of his subjects."[31] For our purposes regarding church leadership and the teaching of it, we should note two implications of the monarchical model for an understanding and practice of ministry. When the relation between leaders and community is analogously reflective of the relation of Creator and creation, and when God is conceived as "above," separate and distant from the world, then the relation of leader/teacher and community is often marked by hierarchical distance in which the leader occupies a level of greater value and privilege than other levels in the community. However, for a leader to be valued more highly than everyone else in a Christian community is absolutely contrary to the life, ministry, and teachings of Jesus. Second, as Divine Monarch, God's action is understood primarily as intervening from outside the world. McFague puts it succinctly: "God's action is on the world, not in it."[32] And because we have received the monarchical model on this side of the industrial revolution, God's interventionist action is characterized primarily as mechanical, directive, and controlling. A monarchical paradigm of ministerial leadership would likely be characterized by unilateral interventions of power over others, imposed upon those of lesser rank.

The structures of church life and governance have not only been influenced by a monarchical theology, but also by economic models. Within a society in which corporations reign supreme and their executives constitute a ruling aristocracy, a monarchical theology will be reinforced by a corporate model of the church. In this context, clergy can easily become identified with the action and purposes of God/CEO and take on a monarchical/corporate persona, exercise leadership as command and control, and use people as means to predetermined ends. If theological educators are not aware of these dynamics and if they are not intentional to provide an alternative theory and practice, then ministerial education will eventually be subsumed within the default and dominant monarchical and corporatist models.

---

31. McFague, *Models of God*, 64.
32. Ibid., 68.

## An Incarnational Model of God

Distinct from the monarchical model of the Creator-creation relation is an incarnational model that is deeply rooted in scripture and church tradition, most especially in St. Paul's characterization of the church as "the body of Christ."[33] If it is true that the true church embodies Jesus Christ, we should strive to understand the church—and its practice and teaching of leadership—christologically, which means incarnationally. Yet, we must quickly add that Christology should never be detached from its Trinitarian ground, for Jesus Christ can only be understood as the incarnation of the Triune God. On this matter, there is widespread agreement among Protestant, Orthodox, and Catholic traditions: "the Church is above all the Body of Christ united to him through his Spirit."[34] This means that the content of an incarnational approach will always be Trinitarian and will always manifest as communion.

Today it is not that unusual for scholars and ministers and church leaders to talk about the church and its ministry as incarnational. But it is still used rather narrowly. The concept of incarnation tends to be limited only to the revelation of God in Jesus Christ, and the implication is that we are supposed to imitate that unique incarnation. That is certainly a beginning point for thinking Christologically—in and through Christ—about the nature of the church and of the world. But if we consult any dictionary, incarnation is a much broader concept. It refers to the material manifestation of immaterial reality, whatever that may be. For example, our faces incarnate invisible emotions, our actions incarnate immaterial thoughts, and our speech incarnates language that cannot be seen or touched. Love is momentarily incarnated by a kiss and more fully through friendship and marriage. Our entire existence can be understood as incarnational for the most meaningful aspects of our lives—culture, history, identity, love, hope, and charity—are invisible realities that we enact and embody, and thus incarnate, to some extent.

That ours is an incarnational existence is even more profoundly true when we focus on the relation of God and the world. If the Gospel of John chapter 1 is right—that all things everywhere are constantly created in and through the divine *Logos*—then the entire created order has the Creator deep within it at every point and at every moment. If Acts chapter 17 is true, then all things everywhere "live and move and have their being in God." Orthodox

---

33. Karl Barth echoes St. Paul: the church is "Christ's own earthly-historical form of existence, the one Holy Catholic and Apostolic Church," Barth, *Church Dogmatics*, IV/1, 643.

34. Torrance, *Theological Dialogue between Orthodox and Reformed Churches*, 5.

Bishop Kallistos Ware summarizes this perspective on the relation between Creator and creation as panentheistic: "Creation is not something upon which God acts from the outside, but something through which He expresses Himself from within. Transcendent, God is also immanent; above and beyond creation, He is also its true inwardness, it's 'within.'"[35]

A *theological* approach to ministry and its education will be oriented not only to the transcendence of God beyond all things, but also to the infinite immanence of God within all things. And because we are being created in and through the divine Logos all the time, our existence is held up and sustained only by the grace of God. Thus, our relation to God is the most fundamental and inescapable reality of our existence. We have no choice whether or not we are related to God. The only choice we are given is how we are going to respond to that ultimate relation: to what extent will we live in or be alienated from the divine life.

We see through the scriptures that Jesus oriented his life and ministry to his primary relation with the "Father" through the Spirit, of which his life and ministry was a perfect reflection and enactment. That is a key insight of Jesus' baptism and testing in the wilderness by which his ministry was constituted as a proleptic incarnation of the Reign of God as he taught and healed and formed communities of disciples doing the same. How are we to understand the church as the body, the embodiment, of Christ? To embody an invisible reality is to incarnate it, to manifest it, to live it out as a limited incarnation of a much more comprehensive reality. Within such a perspective, Matthew 18:20 can be interpreted as wherever two or three gather and live out the reality of Christ's communion with the "Father" in the Spirit, there in fact is Christ.

Christologically understood, then, ministerial leadership is a mode of authentic discipleship of abiding in and manifesting the divine life. In this respect, discipleship and leadership correspond to the sacramental rituals of baptism and eucharist whereby we participate in the divine life and the divine life is manifest in and through us to some extent but never fully. Following Jesus entails a) an immersive movement of abiding in and indwelling the divine life more fully, so that b) Trinitarian communion can be eucharistically manifest in our lives as well as the communities and systems in which we live.

---

35. Bishop Kallistos Ware of Diokleia, "Through Creation to the Creator," 13. According to Bishop Kallistos Ware, panentheism is the "belief that God, while above the world, is at the same time within the world, everywhere present as the heart of its heart, the core of its core"; Ware, "God Immanent Yet Transcendent," 159.

## Sacramental Theological Education

If an incarnational theological education is faithful to its subject matter, then teaching and learning will be constituted proleptically as well. In fact, that is what we find in an epistemology that is theologically constituted according to the doctrines of Trinity and Incarnation based upon the work of chemist-philosopher Michael Polanyi and theologian T. F. Torrance.[36] It contrasts sharply with transmissive or what Paulo Freire called "banking" education[37] in which information is transferred from teacher to student in an impersonal and decontextualized manner, imposed from the outside, as it were. Polanyi and Torrance exhorted us to look carefully at the way we actually know things in everyday life. By studying the way that scientists and everyday people come to know the reality around and within them, Polanyi argued that we come to know something truly only by immersing ourselves in it, and dwelling in its particulars. For Polanyi, "indwelling" is the process by which "we pour ourselves into objects" and "interiorize" them into our personal identity so as to attend to something else.[38]

One of Polanyi's favorite examples of the indwelling nature of knowing is bicycle riding, and it demonstrates the holistic manner in which he conceives of knowing. As a child is learning to ride a bicycle, no amount of book knowledge or instruction alone will suffice. The child has to learn by doing, by throwing herself into the act. Most important, however, for our purposes, is the structure of consciousness in the act of learning. As the child begins, her consciousness is primarily centered in her body and the bike feels foreign. But with practice and with encouraging instructions from her parent, gradually, her consciousness will extend down her arms to the handlebars and through her feet to the pedals. In the context of riding the bike, instruction helps her to focus and be more aware so that she can be more intentional. Gradually, her sense of balance will incorporate the entire bicycle, so that when she has mastered the movement, the bicycle is part of her consciousness, and it feels like it is part of her body. The act of knowing extends her self into and encompasses the bicycle. The more experienced she becomes, the further her consciousness extends even beyond the bicycle into her surroundings so that she can anticipate the road,

---

36. I have spelled out an incarnational epistemology in *The Incarnate Ground of Christian Faith*, 1998.

37. Freire, *Pedagogy of the Oppressed*, especially chapter 2.

38. "All thought is incarnate, it lives by the body and by the favour of society," in Polanyi, *Knowing and Being*, 134.

weather conditions, other riders, etc. In Polanyian terms, she has learned to ride the bike by indwelling it and expanding her sense of self to include it. Instruction is a complementary aid to indwelling by focusing the mind, but it can never replace the participation of the knower in the known.

Indwelling names our participative immersion in something else.[39] But that is only half of the two-fold movement of knowing. We need to name the more incarnational movement whereby the union of knower and known manifests or emerges in thought and action. In our example of the bicyclist, as the young girl gets to know the bicycle (noun) better, she is more able to bicycle (verb). That is, the union of her consciousness with the bike manifests as her ability to ride it. Bicycling is thus incarnated in and through her relation to the bicycle. But her skill is not perfect and does not manifest the fullness of bicycling, so that is why we call the learning process proleptic: it is a foretaste of a much more comprehensive and complete reality. So, here we have two phases of the one movement of knowing: a) an immersion of self into the other, and b) the proleptic manifestation of that union in thought and action. This will be an important insight to keep in mind as we progress to the pedagogies of mindfulness later in the essay.

Now it remains to make explicit the analogy between an incarnational epistemology of indwelling and an incarnational-Trinitarian *theological* education. Both follow a sacramental movement whereby we are: a) immersed repeatedly, ever more deeply, in the ontological truth of our existence: our communion in God. The more deeply we indwell the divine life, the more we let go of the lesser things to which we grasp and the more our lives can be redeemed by, aligned with, and united to the divine life. Continuing with the baptismal motif: b) we are constantly resurrected through redemptive transformation to incarnate more fully Trinitarian communion with God, neighbor, and all creation. In an incarnational-Trinitarian perspective, education is a process whereby we progressively and intentionally deepen our participation in reality so that it can manifest itself in and through us. Within theological education, the following three assertions summarize the approach: a) incarnation is the overarching epistemological method of dwelling in and living out that which we are knowing; b) communion is the fundamental structure and ultimate outcome of faithful

---

39. Indwelling is not merely a particular kind of learning. As a "participation of ours in the existence of that which we comprehend," indwelling is, says Polanyi, "Heidegger's *being-in-the-world*" (1964, x). Polanyi argues that "our whole education operates in this way" whether we see it or not. *Knowing and Being*, 148.

knowing; and c) redemptive transformation in the Spirit is the fundamental goal of theological education for self, society, and the created order.

## Constructing a Pedagogical Proposal

A contemplative pedagogy based upon an incarnational theology strives to foster awareness of the deeper dimensions in life and encourages greater intention to direct our lives and learning so that those fundamental and invisible dimensions are more fully expressed or incarnated in our lives, communities, and societal systems. In short, the drive here is distinct from but not unrelated to an emphasis upon accumulating knowledge or professional skill. Rather, we are focusing on a meta-level of learning—how we are *oriented to learning*—that will enhance how we learn knowledge and skill. It is a three-fold cycle by which we are oriented to the learning process: fostering greater *awareness* that affords greater *intentionality* to *participate* more fully, which then fosters greater awareness, and so on in an intensifying cycle of indwelling that which we seek to know so that the union of knower and known is incarnated in and through us. In what follows we will be concentrating on the practice of becoming more mindful, that is, more aware and more intentional, in a non-anxious manner.

The mindful pedagogy that I propose in this essay takes its bearing from the incarnational-Trinitarian framework in which the ultimate purpose of education is to dwell more deeply in reality, a reality held suffused with and encompassed by God who is constantly creating, redeeming, and sustaining it. We dwell more fully in this sacred reality by becoming more aware of the divine depths within it and more intentional to participate in the divine life as it is manifest in and through us more fully. Informed by a theological framework and a practice of mindful indwelling, I set out to reorient myself and the students beyond pragmatic professionalism. My approach evolved over the years so that now the pedagogy of mindfulness takes the form of two practices that mutually overlap and inform one another: contemplative centering and "drawing novel distinctions." These two practices are conducted in a conversational mode in which I ask evocative and heuristic questions that immerse us all in a deeper and more surprising engagement with reality.

Almost all the students in my courses, and generally at Saint Paul School of Theology, are serving faith communities in some professional capacity, and of those, most are appointed as student pastors. So, they come to my leadership courses practically engaged week to week, and many are struggling with the demands of their ministerial appointment, and they enter expecting that they will learn the most effective techniques for getting the job done, whatever job that might be. My leadership courses do indeed cover administrative functions, missional strategies, and the like, but the very first day I say to the students that the most essential discipline of church leadership is contemplative prayer. That statement is usually met with two responses: an incredulous skepticism by the hard-nosed pragmatists that I am one of those overly pious and hopelessly impractical sorts that boils everything down to prayer, or a flutter of joyous resonance by the overly pious and hopelessly impractical sorts. When I say that we will practice contemplative prayer every class period, some eyes roll with exasperation and some arms rise as a silent "thank ya Jesus." But then an explanation of the practice ensues which usually messes up both sets of expectations.

### Contemplative Prayer

In classes I draw upon two forms of contemplative prayer most often: centering prayer and *Lectio Divina*.[40] For a description of these disciplines, one can consult the resources listed in the footnotes, but one thing is crucial: the disciplines should never be used piecemeal or irregularly. We should avoid thinking about them as tools that are used every once in a while because the power of these disciplines to reorient and center the self lies in our submission to them in regular practice over time.

Every class session is conducted liturgically, whether it is led by me or students. For example, in my leadership courses, we begin by praying contemplatively, either as centering prayer or *Lectio Divina*. More often I use the latter. This time of prayer is the most recognizably liturgical ritualization in the course. But I strive to organize the course liturgically with an implicit liturgical structure and purpose. There are many ways to structure contemplative prayer as *Lectio Divina*, but I have followed loosely a structure that I learned with the Benedictines. We read a short passage of scripture and during the first iteration of silence we allow our minds to explore its meaning. The second iteration begins with reading the passage again. We are receptive to a word or image or emotion that arises from the passage and allow all other thoughts and emotions to pass through our

---

40. An excellent guide to *Lectio Divina* is found in Hall, *Too Deep for Words*. Also, Foster, *Reading with God*.

awareness without grasping onto any one of them. We rest without striving in what has been given to us, and use that word, image, or emotion to center ourselves. After reading the passage a third time, a question orients the period of silence: what is God saying to you about you? The fourth iteration begins with the passage and another question: what is God saying to this group at this time? This practice is meant to center the class in the text, in its meaning, in personal attentiveness, and in communal proclamation. If practiced regularly over a significant period of time, this discipline has great formative power to dislodge persons from their narrowly individualistic and pragmatic agendas and reorient them to a mindful listening for the Spirit's leading.

I build into the class session a period of meditation to complement contemplative prayer and reinforce the contemplative posture that is so crucial to religious learning. At a particularly salient point in the class process, we shift the pedagogy to center ourselves in the moment. Whether it is focused on a passage of a text, the substance of a discussion, or a point of interest during a field trip, the discipline of contemplatively centering oneself in the moment—to become more aware of its intricacies and meanings—helps ground ego activity within a larger expansion of the self. It allows distinctions to arise in consciousness more inductively through mindful observation.

## Drawing Distinctions

Approaching education from an incarnational theology and its correlative contemplative-mindful pedagogy, I use Langer's characterization of mindfulness as the process of drawing novel distinctions. I ask myself the question, how might students best discover how they are approaching their own learning so they can be more intentional about their learning throughout the course and the rest of their education. I settled on a method of evocative conversation by which students observe with fresh eyes to see greater complexity and ambiguity in reality.

There are many ways to conduct an evocative conversation, but one in particular is especially helpful to orient student learning in a course beyond pragmatic professionalism. At the beginning of a course, I distribute a short survey to students asking them to list their primary interests and goals for their learning during the semester. When students talk about their goals for learning in a leadership course, inevitably their answers will have to do with leadership itself. And so I will follow up with their current understandings of leadership. The survey focuses on three main topics that revolve around the distinctions between pragmatic professionalism and a more theologically oriented understanding of Christian ministry: the nature of Christian leadership and its relation to professional ministry, students' spiritual health and identification with professional ministry, and student engagement in the educational process. It is crafted to dislodge their default assumptions and practices.

After students have time to reflect and write their answers, I convene them in small groups and then all together for a debriefing session, the primary objective of which is to lift up new distinctions in their current educational orientation. In a gently evocative style, I ask them to report their responses, and a few times I will ask for clarification of this or that response. I strive to ask questions that are neutral and generic so that students feel they can be open and honest. But I also try to probe their answers, asking them for greater clarification in order to stimulate their ability to draw novel distinctions about a subject that they may take for granted.

Most students report that they have never thought about how their goals orient their learning. The vast majority of students say something to the effect that they want to learn how to lead others, make disciples, grow congregations, serve the community, and many other laudable goals. However, their overriding concern is directed outward, away from themselves, toward professional interests: to learn how to move people, to change them, to get them to do things they otherwise wouldn't. When a student brings up an intrinsic and personally-oriented learning goal, that juxtaposition allows us to explore distinctions between personal and professional goals, and how their assumptions about leadership and their vocational goals change the way they think about and engage their learning. Because students have not reflected very much on their learning, and perhaps because we are discussing this topic on the first day, without developing a high level of trust between us, sometimes it is difficult to keep the conversation lively and substantive.

After discussing their understandings of leadership and professional ministry, we move to the topic of their spiritual health and wellbeing and its relation to ministry. My class survey asks students what daily or weekly congregational activities spiritually energize and/or challenge them: Where are they and what are they doing on a regular basis when their soul is fed? The most typical answers have to do with family, friends, solitude, daily devotion and prayer, and encountering God in nature. Rarely do students

*From Objectifying to Contemplating the Other*

report that congregational activities or practices of ministry are spiritually energizing, enriching, and/or challenging. This disparity between professional activities and their spiritual health is an important area for their reflection because most students seem to assume that personal and professional aspects of ministry are 'naturally' separated from each other.

When I ask about the disparity between the spiritual life of clergy and professional ministry, most of the students describe their understanding of ministry as kenotic,[41] as self-emptying, and they need to go somewhere other than their context of ministry to be recharged and spiritually nourished. However, for many of the students, there is no other community where they experience spiritual renewal and communal mutuality, except perhaps at seminary. In response, I ask whether that spiritual disparity works practically for them personally and professionally.

At this point the conversation could take any number of directions, but the main priority in the conversation is to help students recognize the operative differences between their personal and professional identities: Is the dichotomy between personal and professional spirituality healthy; is it reflective of our communal life in the Triune God? If our ministry should be ordered and structured in a Christ-like manner, then how might the relation of the professional minister to the context of ministry be reimagined theologically, spiritually? Over the course of the semester, we form a community of learning that investigates these topics.

This short questionnaire and debriefing discussion has become a key component of the first class session that orients teaching and learning beyond (but not disparaging) the pragmatics of their professional roles and tasks. During the rest of the semester, the distinctions and insights that have surfaced are recalled so that we do not fall back into conventional patterns of thought and become mindless once again. Because repetition solidifies the pathways of new knowledge, I regularly ask the students how their learning at that moment is not only relevant to their profession, but more importantly how it is spiritually and vocationally forming them. Then I ask how they might change their learning, in light of their insights and plans, to learn more effectively for the long term. In this way, their

---

41. We distinguish conventional individualistic understandings of kenosis as self-emptying from a Trinitarian, communal understanding of kenosis as pouring ourselves into another just as another is pouring herself into us. Thus, within a Trinitarian framework, kenosis is not understood individualistically but rather communally: we give to one as another gives to us.

increasing awareness of novel distinctions lays the groundwork for more effective patterns and practices of learning.

An incarnational pedagogy of mindful contemplation fosters a learning environment of rich and evocative hospitality. As Kathleen Talvacchia reminds us, "The hospitality we seek to create is a form of attentiveness, for it requires of us receptivity to those with whom we interact. When we are receptive to others, we attend to their distinctiveness, seeking to see them as person and not object."[42] As students become more aware of their predisposition toward pragmatic professionalism that objectifies the other, and as we explore its implications and alternative incarnational approaches, we cultivate a community of greater awareness and greater intentionality for the sake of participating more fully in the work of the Spirit which is everywhere and always present. When our learning communities are sites of communion with the truly other, such that our individuality *and* unity are enhanced, then theological education fulfills its role as an indispensable spiritual discipline of the church, for its own renewal and the transformation of the world.

In this chapter, we have focused upon the problematic of pragmatic professionalism that distracts us from the more fundamental spiritual dimensions of life and narrows our attention to an objectifying and instrumentalist ministerial identity. As a result ministerial education is reduced to a mere shadow of its sacramental purpose. However, if God is within and beyond all things, and if our ultimate purpose is to align ourselves with the divine life, then pastoral ministry and by implication, theological education should be constituted primarily as means by which we learn the disciplines of incarnation, so that the divine life can in fact be more fully manifest in and through us. Within this theological framework, I define theological education as an *"investigation of the self-disclosure of God, knowledge of God, and everything in relation to God, which, being properly related to God's own self-communication, is situated in ecclesial communities, oriented in worship to the divine Trinity, and conducted as a spiritual discipline of the church leading to a more adequate mutual indwelling of the Spirit of Christ and the church in proleptic anticipation of the transformation of the world in the Kingdom of God."*[43]

---

42. Talvacchia, *Critical Minds and Discerning Hearts*, 98.
43. Martin, "Theological Education in Epistemological Perspective," 151.

4

# Student Formation through Experiential and Transformative Learning
## Pedagogical Insights from/for Contextual Education

JAMES M. BRANDT

### Telling a Classroom Story

The "classroom" for this story is not typical. While there are class sessions in a room on the campus of Saint Paul School of Theology, most of the student learning for this contextual education class occurs out in the community around the seminary. In 2006, when we revised our approach to contextual education, we made the community where the seminary is located part of our expanded classroom. The course for this story is "Ministry in Context," an upper level course required for the MDiv degree, taught by a teaching team of between two and five instructors.[1] The course requires students to

---

1. The teaching team for this course at Saint Paul has included from two to six persons. I am grateful to all those who have been part of the team over the years. I have learned much from each of them and together we have created an effective learning experience for students. Pamela Couture, then Vice President and Academic Dean of Saint Paul, and I designed and taught the course for the first three years. Since then colleagues Angela Sims, Rick Burns, Ron Brooks, Ed Coy Light, Eric Garbison, Lee Chiaramonte, and Sandra Cox have all been members of the teaching team at various times.

learn about ministry in the community of Northeast Kansas City where the seminary is located. "Northeast," as it is known, is an urban neighborhood that has the most racial-ethnic diversity in the metropolitan area and also includes many people living in poverty.

Reporting on his experience at Della Lamb Community Services in the area, one student wrote in a paper for class "until I visited [the agency], I was not aware of the large community of Somalis and other sub-Saharan refugees that lived in the Kansas City area and what difficulties they had in learning to cope with our society, language and cultural differences. Although I only got a small sampling of this ministry, the experience has changed some of my attitudes and pre-conceived thoughts about immigrants and some of the difficulties that they experience in the United States."[2] This is the kind of transformation we hope for in this seminary class—for students to learn from and about persons who are in some important ways "other" to them. This student was fulfilling an assignment to visit and learn about a social service agency in the vicinity of the seminary.

Student engagement with the community focuses on a "learning location," a social service agency like Della Lamb. Students are required to spend at least five hours on site during the semester to learn about the agency's mission and ministry and about the people with whom it is in ministry, its "clients" or "guests." After a basic orientation, students spend their remaining five hours in some combination of interviews, observation, participant-observation, and volunteering.

Students are then required to reflect on their experiences, both in small groups led by members of the teaching team, and in a variety of written forms, including field notes, a learning location project, and a final paper for the course. All of this reflection requires "auto-ethnography," student reflection on their own internal responses to their experiences. Students are asked to provide a narrative account of their experience, including how their sense of the agency and its people changed over time.

This kind of narrative report requires students to reflect on the attitudes and preconceptions they bring to the experience. It is not uncommon that this process of experience and reflection leads students to changes in their attitudes and outlooks. They are often changed in the way they think about and feel about the "others" they have encountered. As part of this process of reflection, students are asked to indicate how their experiences

---

2. This student was a white, middle-aged male.

might shape their own theology and practice of ministry. In this way a link with their own understandings and practices of ministry is made explicit.

The people students encounter in the learning locations are other in significant ways, often different in terms of ethnicity and usually in terms of economic situation.[3] They are "marginalized other." We want students to gain some insight into the challenges faced by people who are seeking to survive and even thrive in very difficult circumstances. They are seeking to meet needs for themselves and often their children that are basic to survival, such as adequate food and shelter, paying the rent and utilities so that they can remain in their homes or apartments, and getting education that will help them with skills needed for employment. We hope to put a human face on folk who are other in some sense, and by requiring reflection by students we hope they will become conscious of their pre-understandings and how those pre-understandings are affected by the experience.

We further hope that students will discover or have re-affirmed the importance of deep listening to the words of others. We hope students will recognize that people, particularly marginalized people, are experts in their own lives. That folk who are on the margins have much knowledge, often tacit, about the dynamics of relationships and social structures, about how to survive in challenging circumstances. And we further hope that students will take the practice of deep listening into ministry and develop the habit of seeking out members of their congregations and of community members to hear their stories and learn from them.[4]

Students often report that the goals of gaining insight and putting a human face on the "other" are achieved. So, for example, the student discussed at the beginning of this essay, reported gaining insight into the situation of new immigrants and that his understanding and attitude had been changed by what he learned. Because new immigrants make up a significant

---

3. The typical contextual education class at Saint Paul is predominantly white, with perhaps 20% African American and five percent Korean students. Because of the great ethnic diversity of Northeast KC, with significant Hispanic, African American and white populations as well as immigrants from Africa, Asia, and Latin America, almost every student will have some experience with persons who are of a different ethnicity.

4. The importance of listening in ministry is well illustrated by the case study that runs throughout James Nieman's *Knowing the Context*. The case study involves a pastor, new to a congregation, who invites parishioners to tell him about their fears and hopes related to the congregation. As word spreads of his openness to hearing stories, other parishioners seek him out, and he learns a great deal about the congregation. In this case the practice of deep listening contributes significantly to the pastor's ability to work with the congregation and overcome some challenging issues.

proportion of Northeast Kansas City's population and include persons from Asia, Africa, and Latin America, the teaching team had hoped for this kind of learning and transformation.

Another student was assigned to Communities Creating Opportunity, a faith-based community organizing organization. He learned about CCO's efforts to combat the payday loan industry and reported that the experience "taught me just how much collective power people can have to effect change in each other's lives." The student reported being "inspired to think about new ways that we can reach out to each other, and God can work through us to accomplish things that we never thought were possible."[5]

Three female students reported apprehension prior to their visits to their assigned learning locations.[6] They all noted that the presence of persons of different ethnicities than their own and persons who were in poverty contributed to their fear. All three reported experiences that moved them beyond the fear to a sense of connection with the people they encountered. One student was particularly eloquent. She said that she was put off by the odor of a person she was to serve. Then she reported:

> I noticed that her eyes were red, as though she had been crying, and I saw the suffering Christ in her, saw her as God's beloved child, in whom God took delight and for whom God wept as she did. In that moment the Christ in me moved me beyond my refined sensibilities; I moved closer and began to breathe through my nose, as if to collapse the distance I had been maintaining. I found out this woman was living on a porch. That qualified her for a blanket, which she requested and which I brought to her. I filled a material need for her; she ushered me into a spiritual experience that continues to move me and to challenge my notions of discipleship and, especially, of leadership.

Based on these student reports, it seems that the learning location assignment is accomplishing some of its central goals: occasioning changes in student understanding of persons and communities who are different from the students in terms of ethnicity and social class by providing a context for students to process their experiences, individually and in small groups.

---

5. This student was a white male in his early thirties.

6. The first of these women was white, in her fifties. The other two women were Korean, in their early thirties.

*Student Formation through Experiential and Transformative Learning*

## Identifying the Pedagogical Challenges

The pedagogical challenge has to do with the creation of experiential learning opportunities for students to meet and learn from persons who are "other" in terms of racial-ethnicity and economic status. This challenge relates to the theme of racial/ethnic diversity that was part of the Wabash-funded project at Saint Paul. The theme of teaching to racial-ethnic diversity was chosen for the Wabash project because such diversity is growing in the United States, even while significant cultural gaps exist among people in the United States along lines of racial-ethnic and economic status. Sunday morning still remains the most segregated hour of the week. The church needs leaders with experience and understanding relevant to racial-ethnic and socioeconomic diversity in order to face challenges, so student formation in this area is important to the future of the church.

*Overcoming Resistance*

One presenting issue is overcoming student resistance to and fear of experiential learning of this sort. How can we recognize such fear and resistance, allow students to name it and reflect on it, and remove enough of the apprehension so that they can enter into the experiences they are resisting? Answering this question will require attention to preparation for the experience, the experiential learning itself, and the processing of the experience.

In the fall of 2005, the contextual education team offered a new course that was required for the MDiv. "Engaging Local Ministries" (ELM) met with enormous student resistance and, assessed in terms of student report, accomplished little toward the goal that students understand and challenge their attitudes toward persons and communities who were "other." Some resistance to a new course was to be expected. The resistance to this course was overwhelming. Students were unhappy that a familiar and less challenging approach to Contextual Education was being replaced by a course that required them to take more responsibility for their own learning and go out into the community to learn from people they did not know.

Students resisted the new course for a number of reasons. And, as often happens in a situation like this, students with diverse concerns came together and coalesced into one large-scale revolt against the class. Some students voiced fear about going out into the community to learn from persons there. Other students thought that it was inappropriate to "study" residents of the community; they viewed it as exploitative to treat residents as objects of study.[7] And still others found the workload for the class excessive. The course got a bad name among students, and it took several years to turn the tide and achieve the positive responses that were noted above.

Over time the Contextual Education team made adjustments to the course. Especially in the first year, the teaching team spent a lot of time listening to student concerns with the intention of modeling a response for folk who are unhappy about something we do. Over the next years the amount of work required for the class was reduced and the structure of the class was modified to make the assignments more manageable for students. These changes seem to have cleared away student concerns about workload and class structure and allowed us to focus on the concerns related to engaging the community.

In these conversations the teaching team acknowledged that there are risks of exploitation when privileged people seek to learn about and from marginalized persons. We found ways to acknowledge and minimize those risks by emphasizing the need to follow Human Subjects Research guidelines and always allow the person being observed or interviewed to walk away at any time and for any reason. We also discussed how listening to another can be experienced as gracious when the other's story is heard. A person who is listened to and heard receives a message that her or his experience is important and worthy of the hearer's time.

*Restructuring Student Learning*

We made another significant adjustment to the way we structured student learning in the community. In early versions of the course, students were given a variety of diverse assignments. These included a walking tour to observe community assets, contact a community leader, and connect with a faith community in the vicinity. Student feedback indicated many found this experience to be too scattered. So, beginning in 2010, each student was assigned to one learning location where the student was to spend a total of

---

7. See Mercer, "Red Light Means Stop!" 90–100, who discusses the "ethical dilemma" involved in students' learning about marginalized persons. She names the danger as "a kind of voyeurism" that adds to the exploitation already present. In her case study of students learning about the situation of sex workers in the Philippines, she notes that students were aware of this danger and that naming this concern and processing it together with students allowed them to proceed with the experience, convinced that the good in the experience would outweigh the bad.

five hours over the course of the semester, as was noted above. Assigning each student to one off-campus location has provided a more focused experience and appears to have led to greater student understanding of the congregation or agency, its mission and ministry, and the community it serves.

Then, after the first year of employing learning locations, the teaching team realized that an adjustment needed to be made to improve the quality of the student experience. Student feedback made us aware that some of the learning locations did not understand clearly the kind of experience we desired for the students. In August of 2011 members of the teaching team visited contact persons in several of the learning locations and explained our desire for students to interact with staff and guests and have opportunities to observe the actual ministry of the congregation or agency instead of simply hearing about its work. The learning locations responded positively to our request, and in several cases changes resulted in enhanced experiences for the students.

So, in terms of the immediate pedagogical issue—structuring experiential opportunities that can maximize learning—we gained a number of insights. Perhaps most important is the need to make space for students to name their concerns and fears—especially when those concerns and fears latch on to other issues in a course and create great resistance. Admitting that we had much to learn about experiential learning and making adjustments to respond to legitimate student concerns was significant work on the part of the teaching team. We also learned that giving focus to the experience—having the students work with one learning location—was important for a good learning experience.

## Engaging Pedagogical Literature

Recent literature makes clear that the overarching goal of theological education is the formation of persons for leadership in ministry. Because ministry is work with other people, it requires what William Sullivan describes as "conscious involvement in the social networks of meaning and connection in people's lives."[8] Ministers, like other professionals (e.g., health professionals and legal professionals), need engaged, existential knowledge, not only the distanced, objective knowledge required for technical expertise. This engaged knowledge includes practical skills and a deeply formed outlook—ways of perceiving and relating to other people and one's natural

8. Sullivan, "Introduction" in *Educating Clergy*," 11.

and cultural environment. Shaping these skills and outlook is the work of formation.[9] Formation addresses the whole person; it includes intellectual knowledge and technical skills, but more importantly is formation of what Vanessa Avery-Wall identifies as "social, emotional, and relational skills."[10] She lifts up the importance of dialogue in ministry and notes that knowing about dialogue is not the same as being able to engage in dialogue.[11] The latter requires formation of the whole person, including dispositions and character. Formation, then, is crucial to theological education because ministry is engagement with people. Theological education must attend not only to what students do, but who they are. It must form them as persons.

Literature on theological education is also clear that formation of students requires an approach by teachers that emphasizes facilitation of student exploration and reflection over the imparting of authoritative knowledge. In her excellent essay on exposure learning, Joyce Ann Mercer emphasizes the importance of the teacher participating with students in "construction of new knowledge and the creation of more adequate meaning perspectives."[12] For Mercer, the teacher's role in this kind of learning is facilitative—working with students to identify previous experience and knowledge, naming the challenges to earlier perspectives occasioned by exposure learning, and constructing new knowledge and meaning perspectives.[13] The teacher facilitates reflection and conversation, walking with students as they form new outlooks. These new outlooks emerge from the students' experience and reflection; the teacher is a facilitator, i.e. a midwife.

Others use the language of "mentoring" to describe the work of the educator. Jane Utley Adelizzi thinks of mentoring as a reciprocal relationship where teacher is both contributor and recipient. She defines mentoring as "being with someone as he or she becomes acquainted with the world around them rather than telling them how they should experience

---

9. Ibid., 10–11. The language of formation has gained currency in Protestant circles in recent years and has long been central in Roman Catholic understanding and practice. One prominent Catholic understanding of "integral formation" emphasizes that it is "well beyond the transmission of knowledge." Formation aims at the "development of all the human faculties," including formation of ethical and social awareness and a clear sense of the meaning of life. Mario D 'Souza, "Theological Reflection and Field Based Learning for Religious Education," 86.

10. Avery-Wall, "Engaging Difference," 36.

11. Ibid., 49.

12. Mercer, "Red Light Means Stop!" 92.

13. Ibid.

*Student Formation through Experiential and Transformative Learning*

or perceive."[14] Similarly, Emily Click calls for a "nuanced mentoring" that includes reflection with students to establish habits of "consistently reviewing their own actions and [for] building new strategies for more effective [ministry]."[15] Mentoring in the perspectives of Adelizzi and Click involves accompanying students as they explore and reflect on their experiences.

Clearly the experiential learning in the "Ministry in Context" class aims at formation of students as it engages the whole person in opportunities for growth. This kind of learning aims not only at cognitive knowledge; it shapes students in affective, social, and relational ways and can shape the way they perceive others and their situations. And the approach employed in "Ministry in Context" includes mentoring as defined by Adelizzi and Click. We accompany students in reflection on their experience as they review what they have observed and think about ways their encounter might shape future ministry.

Recent literature on theological education also lifts up the importance of experiential learning and transformative learning. Reg Wickett identifies experiential learning and transformative learning, along with self-directed learning, as approaches to teaching and learning that have emerged in the wider field of adult learning theory in the last three decades. What these three approaches have in common is that they all consider education "from the learner's perspective."[16] Wickett believes that all three approaches have important implications for theological education.

*Experiential Learning*

Experiential learning has great potential for student formation related to issues of race-ethnicity, social class, and gender because it can "minimize certain forms of student resistance around [such] emotionally charged subjects."[17] This is so because students have the opportunity to "own" their experience, name their resistance, and wrestle with how to respond to it. Key to overcoming resistance is shared critical reflection in which students are given significant voice, rather than teaching centered on the teacher's perspective and knowledge.[18] Experiential learning, such as that in the

14. Adelizzi, "Artistry of Teaching and Learning," 13.
15. Click, "Contextual Education," 351.
16. Wickett, "Adult Learning Theories and Theological Education," 154.
17. Mercer, "Red Light Means Stop!" 90.
18. Ibid.

"Ministry in Context" class, includes an important inductive moment in which insight is generated from the student's own experience and shared reflection. Because the learning is not heteronymously imposed from above, but bubbles up from below, it has the potential to dissipate resistance.

As Wickett points out, to be effective experiential learning must acknowledge students' prior life experience and understandings. He asserts that "[s]tudents should be encouraged to participate in discussions in ways that respect and build upon their experiences and prior learning."[19] Such respect for persons is consonant with theological convictions about the goodness and value of persons created in the image of God. It is also important in terms of the goal of formation. As Mercer writes, "Only learning that values who we are and that allows us to seek alternative possibilities will enable us to respond to life's changing context."[20]

As Mercer's study demonstrates, experiential learning can have a powerful effect on students. In addition to the respect for students noted above, Mercer notes three conditions that seem important in promoting what she calls "exposure learning." Preparation for the exposure must "evoke learners' capacities for empathy" more than it evokes "a self-protective desire to insulate themselves."[21] The exposure itself must engage learners affectively and kinesthetically; learners must take their bodies to a new place and interact with people in that locale. And in the reflection or debriefing process, students must have resources to help them construct credible alternatives to the perspectives with which they came into the experience.[22] Structured experiential learning of this sort requires intentionality about how the teacher approaches students and about how the experience is structured and organized. Our work in "Ministry in Context" bears this out; we sought over time to structure and facilitate student experience that attended to preparation, the experience itself, and reflection after the fact.

### Transformative Learning

The construction of alternative perspectives points toward the goal of transformation. Mercer's reflections are of particular note here because her project includes both experiential learning and transformative learning

19. Wickett, "Adult Learning Theories and Theological Education," 159.
20. Ibid., 160.
21. Mercer, "Red Light Means Stop!" 100.
22. Ibid., 99–100.

and because they resonate with the work of "Ministry in Context." Transformative learning draws on the work of Paulo Freire and Myles Horton and has gained a wide hearing in the U.S. through the work of Jack Mezirow and colleagues.[23] Transformative learning seeks to facilitate student development of meaning perspectives that are more "'inclusive, discriminating, and integrative of one's understanding of one's experience.'"[24] For Mercer, the goal in the context of theological education is to facilitate student movement toward theological frameworks that are more able to see and name the complexities of human life before God. This movement is toward the construction of new knowledge and more adequate meaning perspectives, what is often referred to, following Freire, as "conscientization."[25]

The key to transformation is critical reflection on the assumptions and perspectives that the students bring to their experiences. What can emerge in the process of reflection is an experience of disorientation when students find their assumptions and perspectives challenged and inadequate to what they have experienced, which Mercer calls an "unsettling of prior interpretive frameworks."[26] This can then lead to construction of new ways of perceiving and understanding what has been experienced, transformation of one's consciousness and of the theological framework employed for interpretation. Students are provided with a supportive and challenging context in which to work through what they have experienced and to determine what to make of it. The teacher has responsibility for choosing, organizing, and structuring the learning experience and then reflecting with students as they seek to make sense of the experience and incorporate it into their theology and ministry.

## Considering a Theology of Pedagogy

My sense of calling and vocation ground my theology of pedagogy in important ways. Having been called by baptism into relationship with God through Christ and called to be a living member of the Christian community, one is also called to a life of faithfulness in all of the various roles and responsibilities that constitute one's vocation. To be in relationship with God through Christ is to know God's steadfast love, to know acceptance, to

---

23. Mezirow, et al., *Fostering Critical Reflection in Adulthood*.
24. Wickett, "Adult Learning Theories and Theological Education," 157.
25. Mercer, "Red Light Means Stop!" 97.
26. Ibid., 90.

know that the joy and goodness of life are gifts of the gracious God, all this in and through the nurture provided by particular manifestations of the Christian community. One is then called to reflection and action—to seek to understand more fully life, God, and human beings and to live out one's faith by word and deed.

My calling to serve in theological education is an important aspect of my overall vocation. The calling is to contribute to building up the body of Christ by walking with students as they wrestle with their own callings to ministry, seeking to nurture them and hold them accountable to engagement in the process of seminary education. It is one of the great privileges of my life to walk with students on this path. The goal of our walk is student growth in theological understanding and their capacity to practice ministry effectively and faithfully. As is so often the case, I benefit from giving of myself to this process, perhaps more than do my student charges. I am often blessed with renewal of my spirit, with increased hope and courage, walking with students as they discern and seek to be formed for calling in ministry.

My teaching role in contextual education focuses on experiential learning, organizing student experiences such as those at learning locations, and facilitating reflection on those experiences. A central theological conviction embodied in this practice is that God speaks to us most eloquently through our experience and that the spirit of Christ is present where two or three are gathered in God's name, not least when the gathering is for the purpose of reflection on experience. Often new insights and new encouragement are generated in the work of small group reflection. Such insight and encouragement is the telos toward which theological education is directed; it provides fulfillment of my calling. And it is directed outward, missionally toward the ongoing fulfillment of the church's calling.

A related theological conviction embodied in this practice is that Christ is encountered through others. Our calling then is to be open to others, to seek to understand them on their own terms. Understanding of the other is often the goal of work in contextual education. When a student goes to a learning location, the assignment is to set aside judgment and evaluation and seek to understand the persons encountered and the mission and ministry of agencies students visit. The operative conception here is that in understanding another, we come to deeper understanding of the world and of ourselves. The result here is growth—including new insights, encouragement, and inspiration. Learning is like conversation that requires talking and especially listening. Genuine conversation includes openness to being changed by the other. So the theological conviction here is that growth of spirit often results from encounter with those who are other. Christ is present in conversation to open our eyes, to help us see and be in new ways.

A final theological conviction is God's preferential option for the poor, understood in terms particularly of the epistemological privilege that poor and marginalized persons possess. This conviction is played out in the charge to students to encounter the marginalized others who are present in the learning locations. Students often learn *about* persons who are marginalized others, learn about the challenges to survival that they face daily. One student was blown away to learn of the situation of an undocumented woman with children who was in an abusive relationship with her husband. Because of her undocumented status and her commitment to protect and nurture her children, the woman found it too risky to call the police and seek protection for herself. Students also learn *from* persons who are marginalized others. Numerous students have reported on the intelligence, courage, and good humor of persons they have met. Students have come away inspired by those who struggle to survive on the margins of society. Those on the margins reveal to us how society works, and how society fails to work. As students see the marginalized, they gain insight into the dynamics of power and oppression at work in our society. For example, students have seen instances of the criminalization of poverty as laws aimed at homeless persons and police raids on homeless camps leave very little space where homeless people can be. The fallenness of society becomes evident when students encounter those marginalized others. We are reminded of our call to be with and for those on the margins. And students often come away from these experiences with new commitment and insight.

A theological conviction undergirding all my work in theological education is that God wills wholeness, shalom for all of creation. God desires that all persons be whole and have all their needs—for shelter, sustenance, meaningful callings, supportive relationships and the experience of beauty—met. This means that spiritual, relational, aesthetic and material-economic needs matter; and we who have caught a vision of God's future, a future of shalom for all, are called to live into that shalom. I am often renewed in this vision as I labor in theological education. Hope begets hope as we catch visions of human beings fully alive—the glory of God.

## Constructing a Pedagogical Proposal

The pedagogical proposal I want to make relates to the current situation and standing of the church. We who teach in theological education orient

Proleptic Pedagogy

our work toward the church and world to which our students are sent. It is evident that the mainline Protestant churches are in a time of significant transition. The "third disestablishment" of the Protestant churches has moved them from a position of great social and cultural prominence that peaked after World War II to an increasingly tenuous and less significant place in the 1980s and following. The mainline has become the oldline. Rendle offers a succinct and insightful summary of the changes wrought in the wake of the third disestablishment. A driving force of this change is secularization and its attendant individualism. The latter grounds a deep philosophical distrust of institutions, which combines with distrust based on people having been disappointed by the performance of institutions. In the political/governmental sphere, Watergate, the wars in Vietnam and the Middle East, and smaller betrayals have bred mistrust.

Similar misdeeds have plagued the church, most notably scandals related to sexual and monetary misdeeds. Distrust based on misdeeds is then undergirded by the autonomous individualism that has grown significantly in recent decades. Autonomous individualism proclaims the right to do as one pleases and not be interfered with; this puts it at odds with the requirements and boundaries essential to any institution. As a result, many people have become disaffected with churches, along with other institutions in society. In the 1950s many people turned to pastor, rabbi, or priest for guidance in life. Today many turn instead to self-help resources, therapists, and Dr. Phil or Oprah. Mainline churches have also suffered losses in numbers as a result of lower marriage and birth rates. Lower numbers have in turn bred a loss of confidence, which has contributed to a sense of powerlessness that can be widespread in the churches. Finally the great growth in the presence of world religions in the U.S. and the growth of those who identify as having no religious affiliation have contributed to displacement of mainline churches from the place of prominence they had 50 years ago. Taken together these changes have put the mainline church on the sideline and made it clear that the church needs significant adaptation to speak to the contemporary world.[27]

The enormity and complexity of the challenges faced by the church call for leaders who can do adaptive work. As Click says, we need to help students "build the discipline of interpretation that moves them beyond instinctive action," so they can be leaders who don't fall back on overly simplistic answers. Such leaders can "learn how to hold communities in

27. Rendle, *Journey through the Wilderness*, 47–52.

*Student Formation through Experiential and Transformative Learning*

sustained attention to issues that can only be addressed over time."[28] Like Click, Gil Rendle draws on Ronald Heifetz's distinction between technical work and adaptive work. The former requires application of known answers to familiar problems. The latter is needed in a more complex and changing context when values clash, when there are a number of variables, and when there is "an ill-defined mélange of factors [is] changing shape as it comes into focus."[29] To facilitate adaptive change, leaders must work with their communities at learning to understand a dramatically changed world and to change beliefs, behaviors, and assumptions as appropriate. Above all adaptive work requires that communities face into their problems and be willing to reflect on what is going on and learn how to function in new ways fitting a changed situation.

The kind of experiential learning done in the "Ministry in Context" class has some correspondence with adaptive work as propounded by Heifetz. Although it occurs on a small and delimited scale in their engagement with learning locations, "Ministry in Context" students are encouraged to face into the situation and identify their own thoughts and feelings going into the experience. They are required to reflect on what they have experienced and observed, name what they have learned and how they have been affected by the experience, and propose how their experience might impact their ministry. In this way the "Ministry in Context" experience models some of the elements required for adaptive work and helps set students on a path toward ministry that can meet the challenges of the church in a changed world. My proposal is that we in theological education continue to pursue experiential and transformative learning opportunities that can form future leaders in ways that contribute to their capacity for the adaptive work that is crucial to the church's on-going vitality and mission.

---

28. Click, "Contextual Education," 353.
29. Rendle, *Journey through the Wilderness*, 35.

# 5

## Immediacy
*The Intersection of Technological and Face-to-face Modalities in Educating a Younger Generation*

CLAIRE ANNELISE SMITH

### Telling a Classroom Story

AT SAINT PAUL SCHOOL of Theology, *youTheology* is one of the Lilly Endowment Theological School Programs for high school youth aimed at theological exploration as well as opening up and encouraging the possibility of vocation within the church context. Unlike the regular seminary classroom, *youTheology* students are high school age—sophomores, juniors, and seniors. They participate in our program over the course of a year looking at vocation, hands on ministry, and a study of the Methodist tradition through theological reflection. This reflection is undergirded by practicing spiritual disciplines.

In *youTheology*, it's the community that matters! This insight led the leaders of our *youTheology* program to reconsider our approach to educating young leaders for the church beginning in 2009. We had decided that instead of meeting on weekends in November and March, we would use digital hardware, software, platforms and apps (applications) to continue the learning between our meetings in August and the following June. The many learning management systems available, including Saint Paul School of Theology's own Moodle site, opened opportunities for a different way of engaging those who participate in *youTheology*'s one-year program. Thus, using offsite digital technologies as a complement to face-to-face sessions seemed the way to go, in other words a hybrid *youTheology*. We discussed these details and implications of less face-to-face time and more online interaction with *youTheology* alumni. These members of the net generation, college, seminarian, and pre-seminarian made it very clear that we had to find a way for more face-to-face interaction than we proposed. It became evident that the two key things about the program that were important to this particular group of alumni were the content and the community that was built over the year. It was not enough to meet in August and conduct the rest of the year online, meeting again in June.

This was in keeping with a discussion I had with a focus group of alumni the previous year. We were looking at the church and technology. While maintaining the importance of tools such as Facebook for connecting, the alumni were clear that communication couldn't stop there. The face-to-face contact mattered. One person made the comment that we have to be sure that we are into people, noting, "You can't find God on a computer screen. The core is loving God, loving neighbor."[1] Moreover, in exploratory research with a pilot group of high school students on using technology to foster missional identity on March 25, 2008, one person asked, "Does anybody talk anymore?" Additionally, research on teens' communication and socialization preferences conducted by the Ericsson Company released in 2012 showed that face-to-face was the form of communication that would be most missed by teens.[2]

The pilot study for using offsite technology for fostering missional identity was conducted in 2008 as part of Saint Paul's Wabash project focus on classroom technology and proleptic pedagogy. It was intentional in seeking to articulate a strategy for using chat rooms and other online forums to engage adolescents in theological reflection and missional formation. It sought to follow God's incarnational model of coming to dwell with us in the person of Jesus Christ in that it would meet teens in the digital world that they inhabit. One of its goals was to have participants select a strategy for learning through digital media. The researcher sought to have

---

1. June 27, 2009 discussion "Research Discussion on Communication."
2. Ericsson Company, "Talking, Texting, Poking and Dating," 2.

a mutually enriching relationship with youth and wanted to learn from them as well as teach in a space of partnership and collaboration. As Mary Hess, a religious educator who also served as our Wabash consultant on theological education and technology, notes, "Our students become in one sense our popular-culture informants, just as we become their religious-cultural informants. They give us access to the digital surrounds in which they move and breathe and have their being, and we do the same with the religious surrounds. "[3] Hess is positing that today's theological students bring digital expertise because the digital world is theirs by default whereas theological educators bring religious expertise because this is their world. We note that while this tends to be true of younger students, it does not necessarily hold for more mature students. In addition, there is a varying level of technological competence among this generation. Nevertheless, it holds true in a general sense.

The research began with one question and ended with another. The beginning question was "How do we use digital technology in educating the younger generations?" The question at the end of the study was "How do we combine the use of technology with face-to-face communication that engenders community in doing theology with the younger generations who have grown up using digital technology?" After interacting with *youTheology* alumni around issues of technology in subsequent years, this continues to be the question we face.

## Identifying the Pedagogical Challenges

The newer generations grow up in environments in which digital technology is seamlessly woven into the fabric of their lives. Different terms have been used to describe these generations. Marc Prensky first used the term digital natives, "because they are all native speakers of the digital language of computers, video games, and the Internet."[4] In other words, the newer generations, teens, and emerging adults, have always known and used these as a matter of course. He later simplifies the term in this way: "By virtue of being born in the digital age, our students are digital natives by definition."[5] Prensky contrasts digital natives with "digital immigrants," underscoring that being a digital native has little to do with the facile use of technology

---

3. Hess, *Engaging Technology*, 89.
4. Ibid.
5. Prensky, *Teaching Digital Natives*, 64.

*Immediacy*

as he makes the point that the world digital immigrants have known prior to the digital age will always impact what they do.[6] Consequently, for many of our students, I have noted that digital technology is like the air and their use of it is assimilated.[7] Pew Internet Research outlines the preponderance and multi-varied usage of teenage and young adult online usage, including social media, as well as the heavy use of mobile and smartphones and their usage.[8] A Kaiser Family Foundation study shows the ease with which the younger generations multitask using various technological media.[9] In many ways, we live this reality.

Our *youTheology* students are digital natives although we need to note that Prensky now speaks in terms of digital wisdom as needed by all generations and the need for all generations to work together and use technology wisely. He finds the terms digital natives and digital immigrants less helpful as time has gone by. They are also what Don Tapscott identifies as the "net generation."[10] Tapscott is referring to those who have always been in a world of digital technology. Larry Rosen makes a further distinction between the Net generation and "iGeneration,"[11] in that the iGeneration has come into the time when devices and programs begin with "I" as in iPod and begin their technological use earlier than the Net Generation.[12] The "I" world is an easily personally customizable world. Both the Net Generation and iGeneration, all digital natives, have grown up and are growing up in a world where technology is taken for granted and are constantly immersed in it. The key differences between the two, however, are that *youTheology* students are both Net Generation and iGeneration. However, this chapter will use the more all-encompassing term, "net generation," to describe them and others of this time period.

It is evident that pedagogical and educational strategies without technology would be a reduction of our reality rendering their relevance questionable. An appropriate medium is necessary. However, in our haste to communicate relevantly there is a danger. It lies in thinking that our

---

6. Prensky, *Brain Gain*, 204.

7. Smith, "To Follow Christ," 3.

8. Brewer, "Pew Internet: Teens"; Lenhart, et al., "Social Media and Young Adults"; Lenhart, "Teens, Smartphones and Texting."

9. Rideout, et al., "Generation M2."

10. Tapscott, *Grown Up Digital*, 2.

11. Rosen, *Rewired*, 13.

12. Ibid., 13–14.

educational pedagogy must completely refocus and provide a digital technologically immersive environment as the key means for effective theological education. This understanding is most evident when we try very hard to get the latest media for our classrooms and/or lament the lack thereof, feel inadequate because of our lack of technological expertise, and/or act as if any digital media will work as long as its technology because that is what the younger generation wants.

This approach is problematic. It shows that we have mistaken the social use of technology and its use as simply a natural way of engaging the world with a deeply engaged and critical use of the same. Without a reexamination of this tendency, we run the risk of missing the importance the younger generation places on face-to-face communication and connectivity, thus placing a low value on what they highly prize. We could miss them. Not only that, we may fall into the trap of what Linda Stone calls fostering "continuous partial attention,"[13] missing important aspects of faith and theological development that a periodic disconnect from digital media would better foster. Additionally, there is the danger of allowing technology to become the tail that wags the dog. Uncritical adaptation does not assess the purpose and philosophy of technology and various programs and apps. Its use is, therefore, unplanned, disconnected, and disjointed. Thus, it does not seek to be faithful to who we are and the end to which we educate. In the end it ignores basic human needs and what young people themselves are looking for.

What we need is a pedagogical approach that honors both the need for face-to-face contact and in-person community along with the natural use of technology while allowing the goals and content of theological education with youth to be the driver in employing digital technology in our pedagogy. The goals and content need a theological foundation. Based primarily on the *youTheology* experience with high school students as well as pertinent writings, this chapter will propose ways of educating the younger generations theologically that combines technological and face-to-face modalities.

---

13. Linda Stone who coined the phrase describes it thus, "We pay continuous partial attention in an effort NOT TO MISS ANYTHING. It is an always-on, anywhere, anytime, anyplace behavior that involves an artificial sense of constant crisis . . . However, in large doses, it contributes to a stressful lifestyle, to operating in crisis management mode, and to a compromised ability to reflect, to make decisions, and to think creatively." Stone, "Continuous Partial Attention," lines 16–18, 22–24. She differentiates it from multitasking where one is trying to complete several tasks at the same time to maximize creativity and output.

*Immediacy*

Much of the literature on classroom technology and educating the new generations is written for the traditional classroom in the seminary. While *youTheology* incorporates some elements found there, it is a program that extends beyond such a classroom. When not on location, youth meet with their mentors where they reside and online with their leaders. We also have multiple sites. Moreover, we are not a degree or certificate offering program. This means that youth are not graded. Thus, different incentives are needed for ongoing engagement when we are not gathered in person.

When *youTheology* students return to their homes in between face-to-face times, they return to busy lives with multiple commitments, including school, church, and extracurricular activities. Increasingly, many extracurricular activities are now graded by schools or done in a competitive way. This reality puts *youTheology* in the situation of being able to get at what is valuable and intuitive in the students' engagement with theological education.

## Engaging Pedagogical Literature

Technology is pervasive. It is a part of the landscape of our lives. It is even more so for our students who were born into this era. As we saw earlier, what differentiates our *youTheology* students from previous generations is that they have always known, been surrounded by, and used digital technology. Edward Foley points out, "[T]echnology is an ancient and enduring facet of human civilization."[14] Here Foley is reminding us that human beings have always employed some form of technology to overcome barriers, interface with the environment, and open new horizons. What is different now is the democratic, global, customizable, commodified, and widespread nature of technology that our students take for granted and with which they connect continuously.

This does not immediately make technology an absolute draw for the newer generations. Neither does it mean that this is the only significant part of their lives nor that it's the only medium they will choose for engagement with the world, their faith, and theological learning. It is easy to get carried away with their facile use of technology. This happens particularly with the digital immigrant for whom the use of technology is external. This is where the danger lies. Thus we need to be sure that rather than using technology for the sake of using technology, our use is grounded pedagogically and theologically. Foley does remind us of the need for a theological

14. Foley, "Theological Reflection," 46.

look at technology when he observes, "While not wanting to downplay the perils of the digital landscape, one wonders what theological anthropology undergirds our various approaches to contemporary technology."[15] In other words, Foley is curious about what understanding of human beings' relationship with God provides the foundation for how we address our use of the current technology. Foley says this in the context of locating oneself as educator and understanding the theology out of which we and our students operate. While not minimizing the possible pitfalls in the digital world, his statement is a safeguard against getting mindlessly caught up in the glitz of all that technology offers and an easy consumption of it as a cure all for educating the younger generations.

Theological education needs to be founded on sound theological and pedagogical understandings, with or without technology. Our Wabash consultant Mary Hess asks, "What difference does your underlying theory of learning make in graduate theological education?"[16] Here she is asking about the impact of our theory of learning on the theological education in which we engage graduate students. This implies that those of us who teach at seminaries and divinity schools need to base our teaching on a cohesive concept of the educational process with emphasis on how learning happens in a variety of contexts. Specifically, a theology of learning is needed when we consider the integration of appropriate technologies in theological education for any age group, but particularly with the newer generations.

Technology does help to shape the new generations' approaches to life and learning by virtue of the way in which technology has transformed the world and helped to create the "Information Age" in which we see the rapid and global reach of information through the unparalleled intensification of technological capacity.[17] Accessibility to technology translates into self-initiated, self-directed exploration, collaborative and customized environments for our young people. For Prensky this means that "most of today's students, no matter what their age or grade level, prefer to take an active role and find things out for themselves, rather than be told them by the teacher."[18] In other words, current students value engaged participation and investigation more than having information given them regardless of the stage at which they are in school. Thus, the issue is not just the use

---

15. Ibid., 48.
16. Hess, "What Difference Does It Make?" 77.
17. Prensky, *Teaching Digital Natives*, 11.
18. Prensky "Digital Natives and Digital Immigrants," 14.

of technology as a category by itself, but how the digital age/information age has refocused students' approach to life and engaging content. Rosen says simply, "They just learn differently."[19] Here Rosen indicates that today's students have a different way of processing information as he emphasizes the disconnect between educational methods and the technological life of students in the K–12 system. Rosen points out that the social nature of their interactions and the multifaceted way in which they engage the world in general, including the use of technology, requires new strategies.[20] Similarly, Prensky notes the impact of technology on how the net generation thinks, referring, for example, to what he calls their "hypertext minds" because of the non-sequential mode of the web and gaming that has resulted in students having a different cognitive approach to learning from previous generations. This means that when students construct meaning, it is often in non-traditional ways. Thus, when we add this to what was said earlier, we find that students thrive when learning through self-initiated and self-directed exploration along with collaborative and customized environments in ways that allow them to investigate in multidirectional ways.[21]

In my own work I have found that this generation needs to be actively engaged in their learning.[22] They react favorably to discussing concepts and new ideas among themselves, relishing the opportunity to participate in their own learning. They are very in tune with classes that mix presentations with discussion, using and creating various media. They show less interest in unidirectional teaching, as in teacher to student, and more interest in communal learning in keeping with the multidirectional nature of their technological engagement.

When we think, therefore, of educational strategies that embrace technology in theological education, thought needs to be given to the pedagogical process and space and how these are impacted by the newer generations' engagement with technology. Moreover, we need to be in tune with what the group of learners needs for effective education to take place. What came out very strongly from our work with the pilot group and *youTheology* alumni is the importance of face-to-face community. There seemed to be two factors at work that would apply to theological education. One was that digital technology was an ever present reality but not necessarily the primary medium

---

19. Rosen, *Rewired*, 3.
20. Ibid.
21. Prensky, "Digital Natives, Part II, 3–4.
22. Smith, "To Follow Christ," 11.

through which high school students wanted to do theological reflection. Another related one was that while technology is a given, a live community of like-minded peers engaged in theological reflection from various perspectives is not. Moreover, in highlighting the importance of the community, alumni have pointed to the communal nature of learning and education as well as the importance of community in faith development.

This emphasis on community is further highlighted by Mary Hess as she draws on the Trinity as community and pulls out implications for education:

> At the heart of much of that exploration [The Trinitarian nature of Christian belief] has been a renewed and energetic defense of the essential relationality of Christian belief and of Christian community. A map for teaching and learning that depicts learning as a process of transmission of information from an expert to an amateur, with a hard notion of authority that reveals itself in unidirectional transfer, does not align with these convictions of relationality. A mapping that demonstrates the multidirectional nature of communication and sharing, however, provides a rich medium for such learning to take place.[23]

Mary Hess points out here that understanding the Trinitarian aspect of the Christian faith moves one from a broadcast, authoritarian type of education to a more networked type because of a basic recognition of Christianity's relational and communal nature. Consequently, the mode of learning is enhanced.

A community that draws its ethos from the Trinity is an open inviting space of unconditional acceptance where one is free to probe and ask the theological questions of the heart. This is rare and not a given. A communal educational ethos modeled after the Trinity provides a basis upon which to respond to the changed learning landscape as well as the needs of the newer generations in theological education. It keeps us from being simply reactive and jumping on the bandwagon of technology.

In enunciating his concept of "partnering education,"[24] Prensky also seeks to move beyond mere reaction to creative education in the light of the technological world our students inhabit. Like Hess, he also indicates that to limit the issue to technology as an entity in itself would be a mistake. He says, "The way for us to succeed under such conditions [speed and accessibility

---

23. Hess, "What Difference Does It Make?" 80.
24. Prensky, *Teaching Digital Natives*, 13.

of technology outside the classroom] is not to focus only on the changing technology; but rather to conceptualize learning in a new way, with adults and young people each taking on new and different roles from the past."[25] In other words, given what is happening with technology and its impact on the brain and thinking processes, to educate in an effective way one needs a new theoretical understanding of learning that goes beyond a focus on technology and involves adults and youth working in new ways and more mutually reinforcing relationships. This then, is what "partnering education" is about. The students take more active roles in learning, comprising some that were previously the province of the teacher, including "using new tools, finding information, making meaning, and creating."[26] The teachers on the other hand, guide the process, monitor, situate it, and give quality control.[27] Like Hess, Prensky calls for a response that actively engages the learner in pursuit of learning and which is less one-sided and unidirectional. Both of these contributions move us to consider the educative space.

It is evident, then, that the educational space needs to be a creative one that facilitates interactive relations and relationships rather than a passive space of single focus on one transmitter and several receivers. This does not happen without intentionality. It is, therefore, a place that is accepting, hospitable, and committed to working with learners where they are while remaining grounded theologically.

## Considering a Theology of Pedagogy

The educative space in theological education is very important because the way in which we understand and shape this space will impact and determine our attitudes, physical environment, arrangement and presentation of content, roles, resources, and reach. Therefore, it needs careful attention so that it reflects the God whom we serve and is relational and communal, liberative and loving, and textual.

My image of hospitable educational space is based on the traditional Guyanese neighborhood as a space that begins with physical demarcations, but which ultimately transcends those physical markers.[28] This happens

25. Ibid., 10.
26. Ibid.
27. Ibid.
28. This section is based, to a large measure, on a presentation given at the Association of Professors and Practitioners of Researchers of Religious Education in 2004

because it becomes a deep, communicative space in which strangers become friends and even family, so that it moves beyond being bound by the physicality of location to finding its meaning in relationships of collaboration, mutual respect, sharing of resources, learning, and protection. Thus, hospitality is integral to the understanding of Guyanese neighborliness. Not surprisingly, therefore, a neighbor is a neighbor for life even when physically apart. People in the neighborhood work towards the uplift of each other's humanity and those in it its ever widening the circle as it envelopes each other's connections. Authenticity is also important in this neighborhood. As we think of technology and its impact and opportunity coupled with its ability to move us beyond the confines of time and space, the Guyanese neighborhood continues to speak to our educative matrix.

*The Ethos of the Educative Space*

Persons, knowingly and unknowingly, long for neighborhoods. They long for deep, authentic, communicative spaces in which real connectivity is experienced. We see this in the prevalence of social networking and texting as people continuously reach out, desiring to be always connected, to be noticed and heard, accepted and affirmed. Henri Nouwen's insight is helpful in understanding this phenomenon:

> In our world full of strangers, estranged from their own past, culture and country, from their neighbors, friends and family, from their deepest self and their God, we witness a painful search for a hospitable place where life can be lived without fear and where community can be found . . . it is possible for men and women and obligatory for Christians to offer an open and hospitable space where strangers can cast off their strangeness and become our fellow human beings.[29]

Nouwen notes the estrangement that has become part of life rendering us unknown to those around, including those with whom we share familial and geographic closeness. He further notes that we are also alienated from ourselves and God. We are ahistorical. This has impacted our ability to be human. Consequently human beings are on a quest for an accepting community that is a locus of fear-free living. This quest is characterized by pain.

---

entitled, "God's Neighborhood Where Strangers Become Friends . . . and Family: a Guyanese Metaphor for Christian Education." Smith, "God's Neighborhood."

29. Nouwen, *Reaching Out*, 46.

*Immediacy*

Nevertheless, such a space can be made accessible and Christians have no choice but to do so. Maria Harris shares a similar insight, but with specific reference to the theological educational setting: "Most of the students I have taught, however, even if they do not articulate it, come because they have a desire for space: personal, religious, psychological, geographical, as well as outer and inner space."[30] Harris shares her observation that students signed up for her course because they wanted an area to connect their total being. She says this about artistic education with specific reference to the course, "The Aesthetic and Religious Education" where students sought to integrate various aspects of the curriculum into themselves.[31] These two understandings help us to appreciate the underlying causes of the quest for connectivity. In addition, they remind us that human beings are more than the bodies who show up in the educational setting and that people operate in various spheres, this setting being just one of them.

As we look at connectedness, it is important to remember in our teaching that the educative space we seek to foster and cultivate is reminiscent of the space we share with God. It is from God that we take our identity and way of being in the world. As Christians, we have entered into a space with the community of the Godhead and the community of believers. Theological education takes place within this context and thus is an extension of the space that we share with God. In moving into it, we come into relationship with the God who loves the world and who showed this care and concern in the death and resurrection of Jesus Christ, with the Holy Spirit empowering and guiding us. We who were "strangers and aliens" have become part of "the household of God" (Ephesians 2:19). This "belongingness" applies not only to an individual member but to all. There can be no longer strangers for all belong. We now exist in awareness of and through our relationship to others. Letty Russell notes that "*Koinonia*, or partnership among Christians, is a gift of the Spirit in which there is a new focus of relationship in Jesus Christ that sets us free for others."[32] Here, Russell points out that it is because the Spirit gifts us, we are enabled to have a fresh center in our relationship with Jesus and thus liberated to an outward, other-focused orientation toward mutual sharing.

God is continually bringing others into this educative space, this neighborhood, ever causing us to extend our reach and our other-focused

---

30. Harris, *Teaching and Religious Imagination*, 147.
31. Ibid., 143–44, 147–48.
32. Russell, *Church in the Round*, 178.

orientation. It therefore requires ongoing openness to God and learning from the Godhead so that we maintain our orientation to God and others. This is particularly pertinent in face of the reality that those who enter the educative process are rarely of our choosing. Frequently, particularly in the initial stage, those who enter are strangers. For example, *youTheology* has an application process, which means that participants are selected. However, there are criteria, which set the boundaries for selection. Once people fit the criteria they are accepted. In this way, there is a limit to our choice of participants. Moreover, when they meet at the beginning of the program, they generally do so as strangers. What happens next is to a large extent up to the leaders and educational staff so that learners reach beyond themselves.

The educational arena is much more than the physical place in which learning takes place. We could pay close attention to its boundaries, layout, and decor, ensuring that these are warm, inviting, and welcoming. Yet, we could by our use of and interactions in this location, our attitudes, and actions maintain a space of strangers. We could communicate that some belong and some don't and thus keep a closed space. Moreover, the educational endeavor takes place in the specified area as well as through using designated distant modes. Consequently, the learning arena needs to become a space that is a neighborhood shaped to a large degree by our relations, attitudes and roles. When these intentionally seek to reflect and flow from the Godhead, the gifts of the Spirit will operate more greatly and we will maintain our orientation to God and others. This will be a neighborhood where anyone who enters, even as stranger, is drawn into genuine hospitality.

### God's Neighborhood

Implicit in the neighborhood of the educative space is that it needs to be a hospitable space that mirrors God's community through which we experience God's hospitality. Letty Russell notes that "[h]ospitality is an expression of unity without uniformity, because unity in Christ has as its purpose the sharing of God's hospitality with the stranger, the one who is other. As Jesus points out in the parable of the Good Samaritan, the neighbor whom we are to love is the person in need, not just someone like ourselves (Luke 10:25–37)."[33] Here Russell links hospitality with unity pointing to unity's inclusivity as against homogeneity, noting that when unity is in Christ, it

---

33. Ibid., 173. Russell draws the term "other" from Thomas W. Ogletree's *Hospitality to the Stranger*.

*Immediacy*

finds its end in extending a hospitality that is God's. She also demonstrates how Jesus highlighted this love for the other in Luke 10:25–37.[34] Thus, although people will enter the educative process from different places with different backgrounds and perspectives, in Christ we find common ground. As we orient ourselves toward God, we can love and be hospitable to others who also seek to learn. For Parker Palmer, hospitality takes on added significance in the face of the reality that learning can be painful and so it becomes an important characteristic: "Hospitality means receiving each other, our struggles, our newborn ideas with openness and care. It means creating an ethos in which the community of troth can form, the pain of truth's transformations be borne."[35] This means that the spirit of the learning neighborhood will be accepting and genuine providing safety for those who are in it and all aspects of their learning, allowing for the new and for travail, which are part of transformational growth.

Hospitality in its purest form is rooted in authenticity. The educative community needs to be one where people enter into authentic relationships with God and each other. In this way, depth of learning will take place. This is learning that will touch us at the deepest places of ourselves and that connects to our most vital needs and desire for knowledge. When we connect with a hospitable space that is grounded in authenticity, people gain a conviction that together, we can achieve whatever specific goals are set and accomplish the various tasks ahead with all working to ensure that all learn. In addition, there is space for new ideas and ways of doing things. Consequently, people are motivated and encouraged by this support to find their own level, create their own space within the general arena. In doing this they discover and share what is new and do their best work. They are helped and empowered to support each other. A community in authentic relationship with God and each other allows us to respond to the deepest needs of the students. This furthers the educational venture. This community is God's neighborhood.

---

34. Luke 10:25–37 is the story commonly known as "The Good Samaritan" in which the Samaritan, a stranger, showed hospitality to a member of the Jewish race from which he was ostracized.

35. Palmer, *To Know*, 73–74.

## Proleptic Pedagogy

### God's Neighborhood and Technology

The neighborhood that is created here, which is really God's neighborhood, is a loving community. This is the type of community that can withstand the pain that often accompanies learning, to which Palmer referred. It also points to a rigorous educative environment. Moreover, this is a community that can withstand the passage of time and place and be engaged productively and supportively in both physical and virtual spaces.[36]

The notion of hospitality is particularly important when we think of technological modalities. Sometimes technology lends itself to more deliberate thought than a face-to-face encounter. At other times, send and enter are clicked too readily and irreparable harm is done. In addition, there isn't the screen and filter of the immediate feedback from facial and bodily expressions. Neighborliness is an urgent priority when we extend theological education into virtual worlds.

We recognize that our neighbors are not only those within the household of faith, and particularly our own manifestation of it, but also those along the way of our physical and virtual worlds. We must be an inclusive community. Authentic relations are desirable not only within the educative space, but also beyond it, in the extended neighborhood so to speak. Increasingly, the extended neighborhood comprises those whom we have never met, but with whom we connect with directly or indirectly online. The strength received within moves out to these external communities because we have enabled participants to recognize a common humanity in which each person in God's creation is deserving of their care and concern. This is grounded in God's love and care toward all persons. It is also grounded in our identity as Christians, people called and chosen by God to represent God as God has revealed Godself in Jesus Christ as we follow Christ and allow Christ to be formed in us (Galatians 4:19). This means that in theological education, others who are not part of the educative core may enter and become a part of it, and those who are part of the educative core will reach beyond themselves.

---

36. *Virtual* is used broadly here to refer to communication and activity that takes place via cell phone and the Internet.

## The Educator in God's Neighborhood

Educating in God's neighborhood requires a collaborative way of educating. Each has to work together for the educative goals to be accomplished, treating each other as respected and valued bearers of knowledge and wisdom. This works at two levels—learner with learner and educator with learners. The focus here will be on the educator who, by example and style of teaching, sets the ethos of collaboration in neighborhood education.

The educator is partner with all learners in the educative space, even as they are partners with each other. In theological education as we share as partners in education, we gather around and learn from the God of our common faith. This goes beyond the simple passing on of skills and knowledge to a partnership of a common humanity sharing space with God by God's gracious invitation. There are various types of partnerships. Some imply complete equality at all levels. Some do not. We recognize that in theological education the educator has the final authority to set the syllabus and grade assignments, although there are ways of involving students in selecting topics and grading in addition to the influence students have in evaluating faculty. Nevertheless, because of the educator's inherent authority, one could make the case that this is not a partnership of complete equality. In this chapter, partner and partnership are used to emphasize the mutual learning experience that is enhanced when all share in common the responsibility for the process and outcome which entails the free sharing of resources of all kind for the good of all.

It also means mutual respect based on our shared and equal status as God's creation and recipients of God's grace. Letty Russell helpfully roots partnership in God's work: "God's initiative in becoming partner with us in Jesus Christ takes on additional meaning. Not only is God the source of the gifts of partnership, but also God's actions provide the model of partnering. In teaching us to become what God intends, God has chosen to join us in Jesus Christ and to make possible a new focus of relationship that sets us free for others."[37] Here, Russell points out that it is from God that partnership originates and it is in God we see concretely how partnership is done. God's partnership with us is seen in Jesus Christ. This was God's decision and this partnership with Christ liberates us for other people as we receive a new relational center. This helps us to understand the basis and center of theological educational collaboration. It needs to be noted that in

---

37. Russell, *Growth in Partnership*, 40.

## Proleptic Pedagogy

most cases one person will have more resources than others at one point or the other. This could be in the form of knowledge or skills or expertise or experience. Although this will often be the designated educator or teacher, there will be times when learners bring more to the table than the educator. In all cases it is important to remember that the resources in the neighborhood are given for the common uplift of all so that all are empowered to live faithfully in fulfilling God's call. God gives gifts for the uplift of the community, not for the individual. Ephesians 4:7–13;[38] Romans 12:6–8, 10;[39] and 1 Corinthians 12:17[40] make this clear. Moreover, all are entitled to respect, access to resources and each other, and all have the capacity to learn and grow. Consequently, there will be a respectful sharing and offering, which affirms and deepens that which is already present and/or brought into the space and/or adds new learning. Thus, teachers need to enter into an interdependent relationship with learners even as they encourage learners to do the same among themselves. It is not a one-way stream.

Since God has graciously allowed the educator to partner with God and God's people, she/he needs to mirror Gods love and compassion, showing respect for all. Moreover, she/he will spend time in sharing space with God in prayer, learning from God about God's neighborhood and then leading in a mutual exploration of theoretical, experiential and practical understanding of the discipline. As Elizabeth Caldwell puts it in looking at religious instruction as homemaking, "The teacher of adults in the church is, first of all, responsible for building a space that values the integrity of the content, the learner, and the praxis—the implications of the Christian

---

38. "But each of us was given grace according to the measure of Christ's gift. Therefore it is said, 'When he ascended on high he made captivity itself a captive; he gave gifts to his people.' (When it says, "He ascended," what does it mean but that he had also descended into the lower parts of the earth? He who descended is the same one who ascended far above all the heavens, so that he might fill all things.) The gifts he gave were that some would be apostles, some prophets, some evangelists, some pastors and teachers, to equip the saints for the work of ministry, for building up the body of Christ, until all of us come to the unity of the faith and of the knowledge of the Son of God, to maturity, to the measure of the full stature of Christ."

39. "We have gifts that differ according to the grace given to us: prophecy, in proportion to faith; ministry, in ministering; the teacher, in teaching; the exhorter, in exhortation; the giver, in generosity; the leader, in diligence; the compassionate, in cheerfulness. Love one another with mutual affection; outdo one another in showing honor."

40. "If the whole body were an eye, where would the hearing be? If the whole body were hearing, where would the sense of smell be?"

faith for faithful living."⁴¹ In other words, constructing a place in which the soundness and consistency of what is taught, the people who are taught and what this means for Christians in living faithfully for God falls to the person who teaches adults in the church. This is also true for theological education for any age. This also reminds us that theological education does not occur in a vacuum. The knowledge, skills, attitudes, and other resources that are brought into the educational space have been formed in other environments. While these have to be respected, valued, and used, there is also the prayerful movement toward what is new, life-giving and liberating that will reshape, add to, and even discard some of the old as people learn to live more fully into the life of faith and harness new learning in fulfillment of the pursuit of an applied theological education.

Just as theological education does not occur in a vacuum, its ends should not be directed toward itself. An important aspect of teaching is facilitating the connection between persons in the educative space and the wider world. This connection is twofold: how we live in the world and how we represent in the world the God with whom we share space and who not only chooses us but also sends us out into the world.

The neighborhood of the educative space needs to be presented as a way of living in the world. The content of what is learned needs to be shared in such a way that the context of the participants becomes part of the text. The text is fourfold. It is the written text, the text of life in the learning space, the text of each others' lives and the text of living in the wider world. In this way, the learning that takes place will be oriented toward the world that God loves. Jane Bozeman notes, "In daily life, the learning community meets the world of everyday people and everyday situations and experiences. The persons in the community encounter the people . . . They reach out . . . The learning community needs to be taught in a way that enables people to take the cross into their daily encounters . . ."⁴² In other words, the day-to-day experiences of members of the learning community are a present reality in which they reach out to those whom they encounter. The teaching that takes place, therefore, should equip members of the learning community to live out the cross from day to day. This suggests a seamless integration of the educative space and the wider context of learners. It points to a bringing in and a taking out.

---

41. Caldwell, "Religious Instruction," 81.
42. Bozeman, "Learning Community," 66.

Consequently, there will be a minimal disconnect between theological education and everyday life and the people who have not had that type of education. Furthermore, because of the basis of our common humanity in the God of love, there can be no sense of being superior to others who did not share this educative space and therefore being unable to relate to them. Recognizing this helps us to avoid pride as we acknowledge God's love and grace that allowed us access to this new learning. It leads us to understand that we have much more to learn and that those who did not share this space with us have other skills that we need to learn from them. As we seek to enlarge the neighborhood and to present it as a way of living in the world, we are able to represent God to the world in love and humility.

## Constructing a Pedagogical Proposal

Doing theological education with adolescents and emerging adults requires a collaborative approach. It means creating a communicative learning space in which students are valued as partners. This community is centered in the Triune God. Its nexus is an authentic face-to-face community of shared wisdom that enables students to reach beyond the immediate circle in witness to God's love and reign. Because it is centered in the Triune God, this is a hospitable liberative space of belonging and creativity. So what does it look like?

The first step in theological education with the younger generations is creating a multi-textured space that is spiritual, qualitative, relational, and physical. It is spiritual as it begins with recognizing the presence of the Triune God; qualitative as attention is paid to the atmosphere in which education takes place; relational as it engenders collaborative partnership, and physical as the arrangement seeks to facilitate collaboration.

When we consciously recognize God's presence and involvement in the educative process, it leads us to remember the community of the Trinity and our ensuing identity. Thus, we are attentive to our reason for gathering as we pause and release to God anything that may prevent us from being attentive to what God has for us in the moment. This is done using a combination of song, readings, prayers, and silent reflection. Technology can be easily incorporated. Recognizing God need not be limited only to the beginning of the learning period. *YouTheology* is punctuated by such times throughout the day as it uses an adaptation of the liturgy of the hours. When I teach seminary classes, each learning period begins with devotions, most of which are student led. In addition, there are many ways in which

*Immediacy*

we recognize God throughout the lesson. I would recommend that these intentional moments of God-awareness be led by both educators and students. They offer opportunities for partnering. They are spiritual times.

In addition, intentionally acknowledging the presence of the Triune God leads to greater mindfulness of each other in the educative space. Care needs to be taken to involve each person in some way in the learning process, knowing and calling each by name, receiving whatever contribution is offered. This will be done in a welcoming and affirming way in unconditional love that makes space for differences of cultures, viewpoints and perspectives. Finding ways to break the ice and set mutual expectations from the inception aid in creating the qualitative neighborhood atmosphere. The relational and physical textures flow from here.

The relational and physical aspects of the educative site are intertwined. Setting the space that facilitates interaction and collaboration signals that a community has gathered and all will be involved in the communication and generation of information and knowledge. It facilitates partnership. Therefore, avoid rows of chairs and tables. What is proposed, instead, are small clusters or small groups of tables and chairs at which students sit. Students choose their place. However, there may be times when clusters are mixed so that students engage and learn from those in other groups. These groups allow for the free flow of ideas pertaining to the content of the lesson and the content of our lives. They make possible the intermingling and enhancing of the various texts (the written text, the text of life in the learning space, the text of each others' lives and the text of living in the wider world). This happens as questions are raised and answered and stories from all texts are brought into the space and connected. It is recognized that sometimes the physical space is limited in that furniture cannot be moved around. Even if the furniture cannot be moved, students should still group themselves into clusters, ever ready for shared experiential learning. The advantage of the physical grouping of the furniture is that when students enter this space, they know immediately that they will be doing more than listening and receiving content. It is also easier to engage each other. In general, based on my several years of seminary teaching and observation of *youTheology*, clusters give a sense of security and safety. They give voice to the more reticent leading to greater participation within and without the clusters.

The content needs to be rigorous, engaging the heart and mind. This shows respect for the learner and the subject matter. Clusters better enable learners to understand how the subject under study connects with where they are coming from, the stage at which they are, and where they are going. These groups will be small enough for each person to be heard and to wrestle with the questions, doubts and fears that arise from engaging new content and/or old content in a new way. Although there will be space for new topics to be raised by learners, guidance will nevertheless be given so that the curriculum is adequately covered. Consequently, discussions will be grounded in the readings and the topic at hand. Once the appropriate level and medium are found, students can be let loose to engage the content and find meaning and relevance for themselves. This can be done by a mixture of presentations and guiding discussion questions from the educator, with discussion being the dominant and sometimes only mode. Note that it is important to make space for questions that students bring to the content.

Creativity is important in enabling students to find meaning and relevance in the lessons. Allow students to create content and learn at the highest level, demonstrating that they have remembered, understood, applied, analyzed, evaluated, and, therefore, created.[43] Give them traditional media such as paper, crayons, markers, glue, magazines, play dough, etc., to engage the subject content toward one of the objectives. In addition, the use of technology is another important tool. Give students the technological tools or allow them to use what they bring. Examples of products are videos, websites, blogs, wikis, online books, digital presentations, sketches, and collages. They can also suggest media to be used. Creative activity is done within the context of the educative space so that it is part of the face-to-face educative process. In addition to creation, technological tools can also be used for research on a given topic. We used this approach during one of the *youTheology* sessions and it went very well. Note that these can also be offsite presentations. However, in the lesson context, creativity is a very powerful learning instrument. Learners are able to bring together what they understand about a topic, how they understand it and its relevance for them, and in this way take agency for their learning.

The educator needs to employ similar tools in presenting the lesson when there is the need to transmit information in a focused way. Prayerful thought needs to be given as to what medium would best support the goals and objectives of the course or program and lesson. When projectors, video players, and other technological instruments are present, it is good to take advantage of the many supporting digital resources available on and offline, which can be used to connect with the reality that students encounter daily

---

43. Bloom's revised taxonomy.

and help them to process in ways to which they are accustomed. Any lesson should be a combination of more than one of the following activities—verbal presentation, visual display, and cluster activity, creative activity. Note that verbal presentation is not a must. In addition, the movement from one activity to another must be focused and organized. This is also a reminder that we learn in different ways and we have various dominant learning styles, thus a variety of teaching modalities ensures that everyone is catered to so that all may learn.

Such a textured face-to-face space sets the foundation for continued community when learners are away from the setting. At such times, it is important for learners to engage in both asynchronous and synchronous contact and activity. This means setting up an online discussion thread, private group or similar space for learners to check in with each other and with the educator to maintain the sense of belonging to the same relational, God-centered community. In addition, set up your own chat room and specify times for more focused discussion.

Neighborhood education is a movement—interiorly and among the various texts. The presentation and generation of content is interactive and multidirectional. It goes from educator to student, from student to educator and from student to student. Like the movement of the Spirit, it is always communal and outward in orientation. It is fluid enough to integrate seamlessly technological and face-to-face modalities in educating a younger generation.

# 6

# Teaching Integrative Theological Reflection as a Way of Life

NANCY R. HOWELL AND F. DOUGLAS POWE JR.

## Telling a Classroom Story

ONE PARTICULAR CLASS SESSION from the course "Theology in Black and White" is memorable.¹ On February 24, 2009, we started class with a cartoon published in the *New York Times* on February 18, 2009. The cartoon read, "They'll have to find someone else to write the next stimulus bill," and the picture showed officers shooting a chimpanzee. We did not offer any comments immediately, but simply asked students, "What is your reaction to this cartoon?" Of course, students were horrified by the depiction, but what struck us was the way in which some of them were horrified.

More students than we would have imagined were horrified by the violence of the drawing and the poor choice of the *New York Times* to print such a depiction, but to our surprise many of the students did not necessarily see overt racism playing a role in the creating and printing of the

---

1. Dr. Nancy R. Howell and Dr. F. Douglas Powe Jr. have taught "Advanced Praxis Seminar: Theology in Black and White" once or twice annually since spring 2007 at Saint Paul School of Theology.

cartoon.² The fact that African Americans have been depicted as monkeys or apes in a negative way and that this cartoon played into that stereotype was lost on many students. In defense of the students, the class meeting was only the third session of that semester; however, the critique of the students who perceived the cartoon only as a poor editorial choice illumines the goals of this class and its role in Saint Paul's curriculum.

"Theology in Black and White" is one of the Advanced Praxis Seminar (APS) classes offered at Saint Paul School of Theology. All Master of Divinity students must take two APS courses near the end of their program at Saint Paul so that they can demonstrate their ability to think broadly theologically, but specifically about praxis. The role of our APS course in the curriculum is to provide students opportunities to apply their theological frameworks to a particular focused issue, as they engage in dialogue with Black and Womanist theology. In our class, the issue is white privilege and the ways in which it is normative in the United States.

The Fall 2011 "Theology in Black and White" syllabus states, "The Advanced Praxis Seminar undertakes the task of sorting out how 'whiteness' gained theological privilege, how Black experience and ideas offer critique of white theology, how new voices construct Black and Womanist theology and ethics, and how white theology is reconstructed in a postmodern Civil Rights era."³ Our rendition of the APS seeks for students to be able to use their theological frameworks, which they have constructed up to this point in their seminary experience, to deconstruct and reconstruct the meaning of whiteness.

The point of the course is for students to develop a deeper understanding of the ways in which whiteness continues to permeate society currently and the need for a theological response. In our opinion, the *New York Times* cartoon offered a seemingly straightforward example of the ways in which normative whiteness still permeates society. Although it was only the third class of the semester, we predicted the students would make the connection between the depiction of Obama as a chimpanzee and the racial history this symbolized in the United States. In fact, we hoped students would be able to engage in a theological conversation that deconstructed why the *New York Times* editors should have known they were playing with fire.

---

2. Obviously we cannot speak to the intent of those publishing the cartoon, but were still surprised by the comments of students who did not perceive it as overtly racist.

3. Howell and Powe, APS430 Advanced Praxis Seminar: Theology in Black and White Syllabus (Fall 2011).

The reality is that many of the students did not make the connection, and we have found this to be true in subsequent offerings of the class. It takes a while for students to be able to apply what they have learned theologically to very concrete ministry opportunities and issues. The process of helping students to think critically and holistically about white privilege is the overarching goal of the course. In our syllabus, we name this mode of reflection "integrative thinking." We write this about our hopes for students:

> The challenge of ministry is the balance of creativity and discipline, and clergy constantly synthesize the issues and needs of their communities and congregations with denominational, theological, scriptural, and ethical principles. Consequently the course emphasizes interdisciplinary and theological methods in service of the church and her ministries. The integrative nature of the course prepares students for the integrative tasks of ministry by using theological and literary texts and exemplars to model synthetic reflection. The course invites students to reflect on formation for ministry by developing their own theological positions on God, humanity, and the Church/church in response to the challenging conversations among Black and white Christians.[4]

The course is designed to move students from compartmentalizing theology, culture, and what happens in ministry to seeing how all are interconnected.

The *New York Times* cartoon challenged students to start the process of integrative thinking by helping them to get behind surface analyses and to see the danger of a seemingly innocuous depiction for the culture as a whole, including their ministry setting. We cannot emphasize enough this synthesis for students who believe they are insulated from racism because they are in locations that are predominately white. This process of integrative thinking helps them to understand how whiteness permeates their ministry settings and the need for a theological response.

## Identifying the Pedagogical Challenges

The pedagogical challenge of "Theology in Black and White" is not unlike the shared concern of most theological education. The broad concern of all Advanced Praxis Seminar courses at Saint Paul School of Theology is to teach, practice, and assess knowledge, judgment, and skills central to professional formation. The APS courses are designed for students in the final "year" (the

---

4. Howell and Powe, Theology in Black and White Syllabus (Fall 2011).

## Teaching Integrative Theological Reflection as a Way of Life

last thirty of ninety credit hours) of the Master of Divinity program. In the last phase of degree work, students have already been exposed to the synthetic, analytic, praxiological, organic, and integrative character of ministry and theological reflection, and the APS courses require more focused and complex teaching and learning experiences as students mature in both the seminary setting and concurrent ministry appointments. The pragmatic goal of APS courses is to equip students to reflect and act as spiritual leaders. In a complex and connected world—inclusive of the local congregation and community—students must be informed by deep disciplinary knowledge (Bible, history, theology, ethics, etc.), but must also be prepared to engage contexts specifically, to evaluate human needs compassionately, and to apply practical theology and ministerial practices seamlessly—without the luxury of semester weeks and faculty presence/support. APS courses are slow-motion simulations of reflective, integrative ministerial leadership.

The narrower, topical focus of "Theology in Black and White" is twofold: first (and with clear priority), the diverse and growing theological scholarship of African Americans; and second, the constructive efforts of white theologians to engage Black liberation theology and Womanist/Black feminist theology. The topical focus suggests that the course is multi-disciplinary, but also transdisciplinary because one access point for learning arises from experience. Because the learning community includes students who are white, African American, Latino/a, Korean, and Native American (depending on particular semester enrollments), challenges with the elusive meaning of *experience* shift. The instructors presume that each student has experience of race and racism, but the experiences are mediated and interpreted by social location, including gendered and sexual identities, as well as rural, urban, and regional identifications. Obviously the pedagogical challenge is how to engage candidly and honestly diverse African American experiences informing theology, all the while negotiating the self-referential filters (intellectual, social, and emotional) that impede careful listening. Sometimes the challenge appears when students insist that their rural communities have no "minority" persons, or when students move too quickly to the struggles of their own family and social systems (poverty, ethnicity, nationalism, etc.), which quickly renders African American experiences invisible. Pedagogical strategies, as a result, must resist tendencies to dismiss African American experience and must facilitate "crossing over" into Black experience with less compromised focus. Ultimately the pedagogical intentions are to facilitate deep listening and understanding first, so that students might subsequently return to their own experience with a more nuanced and analytical perspective—for the sake of examining how they and their congregations are shaped by whiteness and racial privilege or for the purpose of valuing insights from African American race-constructed struggles to analyze complexities, for example, of Latino/a immigration, multiracial communities, or Korean *han*. As instructors, we agonize over whether the learning community we facilitate will generate lasting and translatable wisdom to meet the future needs of the church and other ministry settings.

Even though generational differences and contexts exist, Joseph C. Hough and John B. Cobb considered similar challenges in their 1985 book *Christian Identity and Theological Education*. Within the larger problematic of the relevance of theological education for mainline denominations, Hough and Cobb argue that theological education concerns: (a) attention to Christian identity and memory; and (b) alertness to what the church is called to become in the future.[5] Further, "if the theological school is to be a school for professional church leadership, the understanding of what it is to be a Christian community in the world will be the aim of its research and pedagogy."[6]

One impediment complicates pedagogical efforts to address the leadership skills needed to equip seminarians for contextual ministries in the global church. Compartmentalization of knowledge and academic disciplines contributes to inadequate reflection about the current mission of the church in the world.[7] As Hough and Cobb interpret the problem, fragmentation of knowledge discourages formation of practical Christian thinkers who not only hear God's call, but also mediate that call and demand renewal of Christian forms of mission.[8] Simply multiplying topics, courses, and disciplines taught in seminaries will not better equip seminarians, even though breadth of knowledge is important. Hough and Cobb express concern that simple addition of survey courses in seminary curricula is insufficient because knowledge of disciplines is not equivalent to practical Christian thinking. For example, they write, "We have argued against introducing students to the *disciplines* of theology and ethics, not because Christians do not need to think theologically and ethically, but because to think theologically and ethi-

---

5. Hough and Cobb, *Christian Identity and Theological Education*, 18.
6. Ibid., 19.
7. Ibid., 106.
8. Ibid., 107.

cally requires practice in thinking that way rather than knowledge of those disciplines."[9] Cobb and Hough are not merely raising an abstract issue about compartmentalized knowledge, and they observe that "the most urgent questions we now confront in our quest for justice and peace are not subject to treatment by any existing discipline or combination of disciplines" because even interdisciplinary teams include members who resort to the relevant methods and knowledge from their separate disciplines.[10]

A related challenge is the tendency to approach specific ministry situations in isolation from the global contexts and systems within which they occur. Hough and Cobb note two sources of misunderstanding. One is the failure to interpret local problems as expressions of larger systemic contexts and issues. The other is failure to remember the Christian commitment to salvation of the whole world rather than the privileged few in our own localities.[11] Both points must be contextualized globally:

> According to the images of the church that we propose as suitable expressions in our time of our corporate memory, the context in which our Christian identity is to be lived now is global. The church is in the world and for the world. Our account thus should make clear that the world in question is the actual world of suffering humanity, part of whose suffering comes from the abuse of the remainder of God's creation . . . But we cannot consider our internal history seriously without acknowledging that God's work is for the whole world. To minister at any place in the world without regard for how that ministry is related to God's comprehensive activity is insufficient and can work against rather than with God.[12]

The images of the church mentioned by Cobb and Hough include the church for the poor, the church for all peoples, the church for women, the church as integrator, and the church as a community of repentance (among others), which means that the church must integrate a critical memory of its own injustice with an analytical understanding of the persistent global systems of privilege. The curricular and pedagogical responsibility of theological education is to widen the perspective of prospective leaders of the church.[13]

9. Ibid., 111.
10. Ibid., 43.
11. Ibid., 102.
12. Ibid., 103.
13. Ibid.

Proleptic Pedagogy

The Advanced Praxis Seminar that we teach faces precisely these two challenges: (a) to resist the limitations of strict disciplinary boundaries and (b) to broaden the global perspective of students with regard to the construction of race in the U.S. The course acknowledges the more just moments in Christian memory/history when theologians and church leaders called for the renewal of the church, but emphasizes historical and contemporary moments when Black and Womanist theologians posited criticisms of the explicit and implicit racism in the church. The necessary work of corporate Christian repentance is prerequisite to renewal of the church, but the classroom challenge is how to help students name real world issues and think practically, theologically, and constructively for the sake of the transformation and renewal of the church. When students object that their ministry contexts are isolated from issues of race, the learning community must expand their perspectives from limited localities to the larger systemic contexts of racism and white privilege. Only in light of this broader perspective can the course introduce the process of reflection that moves beyond limitations of disciplinary thinking.

The working thesis of this chapter emphasizes the problem of teaching, learning, and practicing the process of reflection, which Cobb and Hough refer to as "practical Christian thinking." We choose to call this mode of reflection *integrative thinking*, a term we define later in the essay. *Integrative thinking, we will argue, is a pedagogical approach that creates significant learning experiences in relation to racial/ethnic diversity and facilitates student professional formation in relation to theology as a way of life.*

## Engaging Pedagogical Literature

During our Wabash grant project, Saint Paul faculty read Kathleen T. Talvacchia's *Critical Minds and Discerning Hearts: A Spirituality of Multicultural Teaching*. Our goal in the final year of the grant was to think constructively about new pedagogical demands arising from changing U.S. demographics, and our Advanced Praxis Seminar provided a teaching/learning laboratory for exploration of race and ethnicity. Enrollments in the course generated different teaching/learning environments each time we taught—beginning with an all female seminar of white and African American students, and developing into more than doubled enrollment with increasing percentages of African American students, as well as Korean, Latino/a, and Native American students. As the course developed, our teaching partnership

## Teaching Integrative Theological Reflection as a Way of Life

evolved, too. Howell, as white female instructor, and Powe, as African American male instructor, worked from both our growing experience with students and our self-awareness as individuals and as a team to craft a pedagogical style related to the course. Talvacchia's book helps to articulate some elements of our formation as a teaching team.

The thesis of Talvacchia's book, "from the perspective of being a member of the dominant culture in a social context," is that "the spirituality of multicultural teaching entails *changing our understanding about those who are 'other' to us, rather than merely changing our teaching technique.*"[14] Talvacchia posits that the teacher's transformation entails critical reflection about the habits of mind and heart as we engage a spirituality of multicultural teaching.[15] One key premise of her argument is that the integrity and authenticity of the teacher is critical in multicultural instruction, and we might add that for teaching teams the integrity and authenticity of their teaching relationship is equally important, especially when the teaching partners differ in gender and racial/ethnic identity. To further build Talvacchia's argument, the integration of self in relationship is part of holistic formation that facilitates integrative thinking.

The spirituality, which Talvacchia proposes, agrees with critical educational theory that engages students contextually.[16] Talvacchia envisions a model of teaching and learning in which instructors are immersed in the world, reflective about pedagogy, and empowering of students. Such teachers "become integrated persons who bring that integration to their vision of their work."[17] Engagement with students entails many dynamics (individual, social, contextual, political, and systemic) that nurture critical minds and discerning hearts of faculty as integrated persons.

Talvacchia understands that teachers model inclusivity.[18] We could interpret her to say that authentic and integrated educators embody their pedagogical approaches and become part of the content and process of the learning environment. However, no pedagogical strategy can guarantee growth, transformation, learning, or good professional formation for every student, but theological education demands integrated persons as instructors who facilitate formation of integrated persons who serve the

---

14. Talvacchia, *Critical Minds and Discerning Hearts*, 7.
15. Ibid., 4.
16. Ibid., 24.
17. Ibid., 20.
18. Ibid., 56.

church using nearly identical skills: "perceptive attentiveness," "listening and understanding," "seeing clearly," acting differently," and "staying faithful" (the broad formative characteristics explored in Talvacchia's chapters).

## Considering a Theology of Pedagogy

When the instructors are engaged in theological education their own integration and the model of integration that forms the teaching/learning environment must entail a theological stance. Without question, two primary theological concepts shape our teaching partnership. First, our commitment to teaching integrative thinking is rooted, in no small way, in the influence of Womanist theology that keeps us mindful of theo-ethical methodology and standpoint. Our understanding is that theology begins and resides in concrete social locations, and that white privilege is protected whenever we lose sight of the particularity of diverse human contexts. Ethics gains some priority in that theological reflection is a particularistic practice of seeing deeply into the dynamics of white privilege and corresponding injustices based on class, gender, and race, and only then moving into constructive and transformative faith statements. Second, our theological standpoint as we design and teach "Theology in Black and White" is indebted to Black liberation theology. We agree that Christian theology must be liberative and aspire to justice by privileging the oppressed. Attending to voices who candidly name white privilege and injustice, we practice and model a painful process of hearing and observing the physical, social, and spiritual consequences of disembodied theology, which masks white privilege.

Our pedagogical approach in this class is shaped by many voices, but three ideas form the core of how we seek to shape the class. First, we borrow from bell hooks' understanding of an engaged pedagogy (developed in *Teaching to Transgress: Educating as the Practice of Freedom*) to help ourselves and students better understand how one's experiences should be used in the classroom.[19] We talked earlier in the chapter about the challenge many students face in listening to an experience that is very different from and often contradicts their worldviews. One of the ways we address this issue in our pedagogical approach is by building on bell hooks' engaged pedagogy. Hooks argues,

---

19. hooks, *Teaching to Transgress*, 21.

> When education is the practice of freedom, students are not the only ones who are asked to share, to confess. Engaged pedagogy does not seek simply to empower students. Any classroom that employs a holistic model of learning will also be a place where teachers grow, and are empowered by the process. That empowerment cannot happen if we refuse to be vulnerable while encouraging students to takes risks. Professors who expect students to share confessional narratives but who are themselves unwilling to share are exercising power in a manner that could be coercive.[20]

We, as instructors, are intentional about the ways in which we share our narratives with the class and listen to one another both inside and outside of the class. For example, we meet weekly to plan each class session, and during those meetings, we listen to each other to hear how our experiences may illuminate or detract from what we hope to achieve during that class session. During the actual class sessions, we do the same thing not only with ourselves, but with students so that all are vulnerable, but also encouraged to take risks.

One of the dangers of this pedagogical strategy is a tendency by some simply to appropriate African American experience and make it their own. Emilie Townes warns us about such appropriation in, "Appropriation and Reciprocity in Womanist/Mujerista/Feminist Work." Townes writes,

> what we must be about as we approach one another's work
>     is care-filled listening and observing and engagement
> this takes time
>     energy
>     resources
>     fortitude
>     and a stout will-to-comprehend
> the voice is salient
>     yet this is not a disembodied voice
>     but one in which rich traditions and histories
>     have shaped it
>     (and continue to be renewed and transformed)
> it is a voice from a particular culture
>     whose integrity and worth must be respected
> if we rush in too quickly
>     with our tools of correct analysis
>     and sisterly solidarity
> the voice we will hear is our own echo

20. Ibid.

## Proleptic Pedagogy

> a distortion of the original
> but dolby in sound[21]

Townes agrees with the pedagogical strategy of listening, but she cautions that we must be mindful of the way we listen. Listening in such a way that we simply seek to correct what we perceive as wrong is just another way of hearing our own experience. In "Theology in Black and White," our approach to every class is to prepare in such a way that we carefully listen to the text, students, and each other, making ourselves open and vulnerable to what is being argued. We also respect the voice of the text, students and each other in such a way that we do not simply privilege a particular experience "through the back door" (speaking figuratively).

For us, an engaged pedagogical strategy requires preparing for every class in such a way that we are as vulnerable as the students and not simply dictators of information. Engaged pedagogy means sharing parts of our narrative, but doing so in a way that furthers the theological dialogue. It means remembering that our solutions to what we read or what is presented may be another form of privileging our own experiences. Using this strategy has helped us to be intentional about the construction of the course, as well as every class session during the semester.

Second, spirituality has to be shaped in community. This statement seems fairly obvious on the surface, but we believe nurturing spirituality is more challenging than most think. For example, most students read the syllabus and develop a check list that looks something like this: read weekly assignments, discuss texts in class, write a paper, and present the paper in the last few weeks of class.[22] Certainly many of the activities listed are achieved in community, class discussions, and oral presentations. While these activities occur in community, they do not communicate what we are suggesting for a communal spirituality.

Although bell hooks' book, *Teaching to Transgress* is over fifteen years old, her ideas are still timely in defining the challenge of moving beyond constricted pedagogical paradigms. One such paradigm she invites us to transgress is class preparation designed to deliver information.[23] Hooks debunks the notion that we have to teach disengaged concepts intended for student

---

21. Townes, "Appropriation and Reciprocity in Womanist/Mujerista/Feminist Work," 116.

22. We have no scientific study to back this claim, except observation from the first day of class and student questions pertaining to the syllabus.

23. hooks, *Teaching to Transgress*, 129.

acquiescence. Although the classroom makes up a community, the paradigm simply operates with a collection of individuals functioning separately, so we can check things off a list included in the syllabus or class plan.

Hooks' solution to the problem of mere delivery of information is structured around dialogue. She writes, "To engage in dialogue is one of the simplest ways we can begin as teachers, scholars, and critical thinkers to cross boundaries, the barriers that may or may not be erected by race, gender, class, professional standing, and a host of other differences."[24] In "Theology in Black and White," we build on hooks' notion in the way we seek to understand spirituality in community.

The class is constructed as a theological dialogue among the texts, students, and professors. We prepare for each class thinking about how all of the dialogue partners can transgress boundaries and think about spirituality differently within the teaching/learning community. For example, the paper students write for the class is one that they develop for the entire semester as they receive constant feedback from classmates and professors. The paper encapsulates the ongoing theological dialogue we seek to embody for the course.

We begin the dialogue process the first day of class by having students state aloud what interests them about African American theology. We build on this initial dialogue every week through the students engaging the texts, each other, and us. This approach means we are a part of the dialogue and also are being informed by the conversation. We are co-participants, with everyone else in the class, in the process of transgressing boundaries that constrict community. As a part of this pedagogical strategy, we share a piece of our scholarship during the course, not simply as information, but so that students can give us the same feedback that everyone else in the community receives while writing the seminar paper.[25]

What we have learned by this approach is that developing a community where individuals are encouraged to transgress boundaries is challenging. We continue to structure the class as a whole to encourage transgressing boundaries in order to develop a communal spirituality and

---

24. Ibid., 130.

25. We realize that having a prepared written piece is different than having to construct a paper during the semester, but do believe the process of engaging the professors' writing is similar to what students experience in the community. The process of criticizing and responding to the instructors' writing and thought permits students to practice modes of critical thinking, which they can apply to their own work in writing the seminar paper and in responding to other students' papers.

prepare each class to be an ongoing theological dialogue toward this end. The payoff from developing a communal spirituality is that no single voice informs the entire conversation—and the same spirit is encapsulated in the construction of the student seminar papers. Several voices are a part of the final product making all of us participants in a way that goes beyond completing a check list of assignments.

Third, African American literature is a window into integrative thinking. Individuals, such as Katie Cannon, have written about the importance of African American literature for engaging theo-ethics.[26] Simply using African American literature in class is not something new. What we do believe is somewhat unique is using the literature as a pedagogical strategy to provide a window into integrative thinking.

In some ways, all of the pedagogical strategies mentioned above reinforce integrative thinking, but the use of African American literature to prepare for the course encourages us and students to think about integration differently. For example, *The Color Purple* by Alice Walker is the first text read in the course because we find that the novel helps us to examine theological categories and practical issues related to race, gender and sexuality, and then the book moves us toward understanding what it means to embody theology as a way of life.

Engaging these themes in literature as part of a narrative helps us to prepare students who often perceive theology as disembodied from their narrative lives. Reading literature prepares us to think about the way in which theological categories and such issues as race intersect in our own lives daily helping us to frame our experiences in ways that open up theological dialogue. Using literature helps us to think creatively about these intersections instead of beginning with standard textual starting points. With literature, experience meets experience—that is, the experiences of fictional characters meet the experiences of students—so that the story creates an embodied moment when students must confront the narratives of others and their relevance and transformative power for members of the teaching/learning community.

We draw on literature not only because it is one of the main resources for Black and Womanist theologians, but because literature, such as *The Color Purple*, illustrates integrative thinking in a holistic manner. In thinking about how to teach integration so that reflection is not merely a mechanical exercise, we propose that showing how Alice Walker, Zora Neale

---

26. See, for example Cannon, *Katie's Canon*.

*Teaching Integrative Theological Reflection as a Way of Life*

Hurston, James Baldwin, or Charles Johnson develop characters and stories exemplifies the principle that theology is not compartmentalized from the rest of life. In fact, theology is a way of understanding life at its core. Theology as a way of life is the spirituality central to our clarity about course preparation and teaching because the principle functions as the central integrative concept in the course.

## Constructing a Pedagogical Proposal

The idea of theology as a way of life is fundamental for the pedagogy that assists us in engaging and practicing integrative thinking. We first started using this idea when we applied and received a Yale teaching award, and the process of application for the award led us to reflect on how one bridges thinking, acting, and being in the life of faith.[27] Miroslav Volf defines *theology as a way of life*: "*at the heart of every good theology lies not simply a plausible intellectual vision but more importantly a compelling account of a way of life, and that theology is therefore best done from within the pursuit of this way of life.*"[28] Volf's definition describes what we seek to accomplish in the course and in each class meeting because the principle helps us to embody and explain the movement from compartmentalization of Christian life to more holistic spirituality.

When we are working on the different aspects of our theology of pedagogy—engaged pedagogy, communal spirituality, and African American literature to promote integrative thinking—foremost is theology as a way of life. We reject pedagogy that simply teaches students disconnected theological concepts and disembodied practices. We participate with students in developing a way of understanding life at its core, with all the integrity that faith affords.

The pedagogical device that pulls aspects of our course together we call *practices of justice*. In thinking about what we teach and what it means for theology to be a way of life, our interpretation of practices of justice is indebted to Volf's reflection on the coinherence of Christian beliefs and practices. Volf argues that "beliefs *as beliefs* entail practical commitments. These commitments may need to be explicated so as to become clear, or

---

27. We submitted the "Theology in Black and White" course to the Yale Center for Faith and Culture in application for a Faith as a Way of Life Theological Education Renewal Award, which we received in 2007.

28. Volf, "Theology for a Way of Life," 247.

they may need to be connected to specific issues in concrete situations, but they don't need to be *added* to the beliefs; they inhere in the beliefs."[29] Because "practices are essentially belief-shaped, and beliefs are essentially practice-shaping," right practices "*are likely* to open persons for insights into beliefs to which they would otherwise be closed."[30] The intimately fitted relationship of beliefs and practices evokes a way of life distinctively Christian in resonance with divine action and engagement with the world.[31] We define practice of justice in the syllabus as "a particular action, such as use of liberating language, works of resistance to racism, honesty in truth-telling, courage in moral agency, spirituality of wholeness, commitment to survival, and openness to listening. Practices of justice are intentional spiritual practices expressing overt signs of justice-making."[32] Alongside theological reflection, practices of justice are the ways in which we bring all of who we are as Christians to bear upon issues we face daily in life.

Volf names the importance of thinking differently about theology abstracted from lived experience when he warns, "The scholarly interests of theologians then fail to match the realities of the people in the pew and on the streets."[33] His point is that theology should speak to the daily issues of life that we all face and not simply be an exercise in debating "conceptual difficulties."[34] We participate with students in not overlooking the daily issues of life by focusing on practices of justice.

The practice of justice takes into account the issue at hand; it requires thinking theologically about the issue; and it moves us to consider a response that promotes justice for all parties involved. This is particularly important when dealing with race, gender, and sexuality issues that tend to be so polarized in our society. For example, consider an homogeneous Anglo congregation that has not given much thought to its use of language that equates dark with negative and light with good. A responsive and constructive ministry might be a Bible study that discusses how concepts we take for granted in every day liturgies may in fact reinforce racism. The engagement of the congregation might include thinking about how we maintain the

---

29. Ibid., 253.

30. Ibid., 254, 257.

31. Ibid., 255.

32. Howell and Powe, APS 430 Advanced Praxis Seminar: Theology in Black and White Syllabus (Fall 2011).

33. Volf, "Theology for a Way of Life," 246.

34. Ibid., 247.

power and significance of the liturgies, but change some of the language we use that reinforces the goodness of light at the expense of darkness. A number of practices of justice might be used to integrate thinking about the dichotomous liturgical language. One practice of justice might be truth telling as believers benefitting from white privilege face the problem of liturgies implying that blackness is negative. Another direct practice of justice might be deconstructing language and confronting the embedded concepts in words that maintain white privilege.

The goal is for students to be able to articulate their practices of justice clearly, illustrating that they are able to move beyond compartmentalizing. We believe the ability to do this fosters in each student thinking about theology as a way of life—rather than making theological reflection an inconvenient bother on the way toward some other goal. The uniqueness of theological education is that it gives one a different perspective on life that should move a community toward wholeness.

We propose that attention to practices of justice facilitates integrative thinking in pedagogies focused on theology as a way of life. Practices of justice function as integrative metaphors, images, or concepts that evoke and sharpen expression of the multidisciplinary, transdisciplinary, relational, praxiological, and spiritual dimensions of theology as a way of life—not as separate compartments of theological reflection, but as aspects that cohere and exist as one. Integrative thinking requires focused pedagogy that returns to the practices of justice in a variety of ways. Not only do we begin our course with discussion of the meaning of *practice of justice*, but we also begin each class session by naming a practice of justice and then reading a passage of theology, poetry, prose, or scripture that exemplifies the practice. For example, the excerpt from towne's poem quoted earlier in the chapter is an illustration of engaged listening as a practice of justice. Reading novels by Alice Walker, Charles Johnson, Zora Neale Hurston, and James Baldwin creates occasions for us to use practices of justice to interpret the characters or events, and students often propose and name diverse practices that express how they encounter the literature. Writing assignments require that students select (and even invent and name) a practice of justice that best expresses how their constructive theologies, congregational needs, personal experiences, and theological education come together to suggest a relevant application to ministry in a concrete setting. For example, one of our students devised *lament* as a practice of justice to integrate comparison of Walter Brueggemann's and Delores Williams' hermeneutics with consideration of theodicy and the doctrine of God and reflections on reconciliation as a complex ministry within congregations. Our course engages theological texts through practices of justice. For example, as an interpretation of Delores Williams' *Sisters in the Wilderness,* we explore how survival functions as a practice of justice to integrate scripture, history, literature, theology, and experience. As we read Howard Thurman's *Jesus and the Disinherited,* we name his practice of justice as truth-telling in contrast to the disintegrative "hounds of hell" (fear, hate, and deception), which Thurman sees as impediments to reconciliation.

The ambitions and challenges of our Advanced Praxis Seminar require rigorous course design and implementation. The concept holding all these threads in tension is *integrative thinking,* which functions as a methodological approach for analysis of white privilege and race. Our goal is for students to acquire and practice the skill of integrative thinking, and we sincerely hope and anticipate that this approach is applicable to issues in addition to Black and white Christian dialogue.

L. Dee Fink is an appropriate conversation partner as we reflect on integrative course design under the assumption that course design should model integrative thinking. Fink is author of *Creating Significant Learning Experiences: An Integrated Approach to Designing College Courses.* Fink addresses the problem of inadequate teaching practices that result in ineffective learning. He reports that evaluative data indicate "that higher education is currently turning out graduates who neither have good general knowledge nor know how to engage in the kind of complex thinking and reasoning that society needs today."[35] Fink notes that faculty desire and expect high-level learning form students, but use pedagogical approaches that are contradictory to creating significant learning.[36] Instructors tend to focus on content-oriented, lecture-based pedagogy, which aspires to "memorized knowledge" among students.[37] While teaching/learning is becoming more active in character and pedagogical approaches (including online learning) are more diverse, when lecture methods are used:

> A long history of research indicates lecturing has limited effectiveness in helping students

---

35. Fink, *Creating Significant Learning Experiences,* 3.
36. Ibid.
37. Ibid., 2.

- Retain information after a course is over.
- Develop an ability to transfer knowledge to novel situations.
- Develop skill in thinking or problem solving.
- Achieve affective outcomes, such as motivation for additional learning or a change in attitude.[38]

Both students and faculty have inspiring aspirations for the classroom; however, Fink's experience in working with faculties is that their creative, imaginative visions for teaching/learning are not evident in their ordinary classroom teaching practices.[39]

What relevance does Fink's criticism of higher education have for theological education? First, seminaries enroll students who are products of uninspired college teaching. Given the average age of seminarians, our students may not have retained knowledge we consider prerequisites for advanced theological study nor are they enculturated to newer modes of thinking and learning—although among our students are many notable exceptions. Second, seminary faculties sometimes default to lecture-based pedagogies laced with discussion and visual presentations. In spite of appreciation for the pedagogical insights of Paulo Freire, bell hooks, Katie Cannon, etc., seminary faculty may still employ the banking model of learning in hope that our deposits of knowledge will benefit the church as clergy alumni/ae make appropriate and timely withdrawals.

Fink understands integration as one aspect of significant learning experiences, and *integration* is the kind of learning that equips students to "learn how to connect and relate various things to each other."[40] Integration occurs in many ways, but Fink offers three examples of integration. First, interdisciplinary learning is critical for discerning how to "connect and integrate different kinds of information, perspectives, and methods of inquiry and analysis," which prepares students to engage complex issues more holistically.[41] Second, learning communities are places of integration because of the kinds of relationships created among students, instructors, and course subject matter.[42] Third, integration may entail building the

---

38. Ibid., 3.
39. Ibid., 8.
40. Ibid., 42.
41. Ibid., 43.
42. Ibid.

connections between academics and other aspects of student life.[43] While this third mode of integration explores the relevance of information to the student's life, Fink situates integration with other crucial modes of significant learning, such as human dimensions (which explore constructive relationships with self and others, broader concepts of others, emotional intelligence, and reciprocity with others),[44] caring (which develops student affective connections to values and ideas),[45] or application (which bridges skills, critical thinking, and creative thinking).[46] What Fink hopes to accomplish as significant learning, our Advanced Praxis Seminar hopes to achieve by using integrative thinking to instill theology as a way of life.

Our pedagogical proposal is that *integrative thinking is a pedagogical approach that creates significant learning experiences in relation to racial/ethnic diversity and facilitates student professional formation in relation to theology as a way of life.* Integrative thinking is a process of weaving together the threads of one's life, thought, and ministry. At one level, integrative thinking is multidisciplinary theological reflection, which all forms of ministry require as we bring together the disciplines learned in seminary education to address the needs of congregations and communities. At another level, integrative thinking is the responsive and deep listening that transforms who we are when we truly hear and understand the experiences of those who confront us with concrete lived reality—in some important cases, with the systemic effects of white privilege. At a third level, integrative thinking is the deep encounter with self, which is nuanced by theological breadth and social, interpersonal texture. The encounter with others (through thought and experience) is transdisciplinary as we ground our learning in experience, but also is praxiological as we formulate how our behaviors and actions are transformed in meaningful engagement with diverse persons and ideas. Integrative thinking is engaged and embodied as an intellectual and mindful spirituality practiced by living, acting, being and becoming, listening, thinking, and responding. Integrative thinking might even be termed a spiritual gift of those who are called to ministry and understand the integrity of Christian vocation as holistic and relational.

---

43. Ibid., 44.
44. Ibid., 44–48.
45. Ibid., 48.
46. Ibid., 38–42.

# 7

# Pedagogical Issues in Theological Education for Diverse Peoples and Divergent Thinkers

Sondra Higgins Matthaei with Jami Moss

## Telling a Classroom Story

MY SPRING 2012 SPIRITUAL direction class was more racially and ethnically diverse than usual. It also was small enough to be a seminar style class with leadership provided by teacher and students alike. More by instinct than by intention, two of the texts I chose were polar opposites in terms of addressing spiritual direction. One clearly approached the topic from a white male's perspective with no evident awareness of any other perspectives, and the other was team-written text by an artist and a dancer.[1] The students from diverse racial/ethnic backgrounds and cultures, as well as the women students, struggled with the former and found significant connection with the latter. In addition, the use of the arts in class assignments and discussion helped us articulate a deeper theological and theoretical understanding of a ministry of spiritual direction.

A critical moment happened in this class for Rev. Jami Moss, a student of Creek origin and a licensed pastor in the Oklahoma Indian Missionary

1. Paintner and Beckman, *Awakening the Creative Spirit*.

Proleptic Pedagogy

Conference, who described her experience in this way: "We were talking about how the text was constructed from a white male's analytical viewpoint. I couldn't understand how the author came to some of the summations that were discussed in his book. As a result, I felt like the way I understood things was invalid and had no significance."[2] Additional comments clearly reflected that this type of discouragement was a common occurrence for Rev. Moss in her seminary classes. At this point, I intervened and asked the class whether they heard what was said behind the words. We had just discussed global and analytic thinking so I was able to point out that Rev. Moss was operating out of her strength in seeing the relationships and connections between ideas and issues, a global and connected way of thinking common to her Creek heritage in contrast to the author's analytical perspective. It was a transforming moment for all of us as Rev. Moss realized she did have something of value to contribute to our discussions. In a later reflection, she wrote,

> I felt like the way I understood things to be was invalid and had no significance. However, in reality as revealed through our class discussion, I simply learn and think differently. When a global thinker like me is systemically and systematically assessed by analytical thinkers, it causes me to feel incompetent. Academically, I am a round peg that is trying to fit into a square hole. I feel like global thinking is not as common as analytical thinking. This may not be true, but this is what I feel. I feel global thinkers like me are assessed according to analytical thinking patterns and that causes a struggle in my understanding as a global thinker. This struggle then leads to a consideration of who is right or wrong in the mind of the global thinker. I have come to the understanding that there should never be a struggle of who is right or wrong but that there are different points of view and at times global and analytical thinkers should be willing to disagree without being judged as right or wrong.

In this reflection, Rev. Moss is sharing her feelings that there is an assumption about the right way of expressing ideas in most classroom discussions. Her comments demonstrate frustration with the experience that her cultural way of reflecting on ideas is generally not heard or accepted in seminary

---

2. Rev. Jami Moss is a student of Creek origin at Saint Paul School of Theology in Kansas City, Missouri, and licensed local pastor in the Oklahoma Indian Missionary Conference of The United Methodist Church serving Lawrence Indian United Methodist in Lawrence, Kansas, and Kansas City Native American Ministries. Used by permission.

classes, leaving her to conclude that her ideas are wrong and invalid. If she wants to be heard rather than dismissed without consideration, then she needs to use only an analytical way of thinking and expressing herself. Rev. Moss is making a compelling case for the problem that is created in much of theological education for diverse peoples and divergent thinkers when analytical thinking and disregard for the values and worldviews of cultural heritage become the norm in pedagogy and assessment.

## Identifying the Pedagogical Challenges

This issue is at the heart of my examination of pedagogy in this chapter. As one who was educated at Saint Paul School of Theology and now has taught at this seminary for twenty-five years, the values of multicultural diversity and social justice are deeply ingrained in my identity and practice in a ministry of teaching. As a Christian educator, I have long been involved in discussions of pedagogy in the academy and in the local church. One of my gifts in teaching is the ability to work with students who come from diverse cultural and educational backgrounds, recognizing that my learning curve has spanned more than thirty years. In this chapter, I use my research on pedagogy in theological education that would be hospitable for Native Americans developed for Saint Paul's Wabash grant on "proleptic pedagogy," as well as my experience with Native Americans in theological education to explore pedagogical issues related to contrasting worldviews and ways of thinking and learning. I recognize that I have much to overcome in my understanding since I am an older Caucasian female Christian who has been educated in the Western European tradition, but I have learned much from my Native American students and colleagues over the years. This classroom experience continues to push my awareness of the unique gifts that students from Native American cultures bring to our classrooms and to church leadership if we address the barriers created by our lack of knowledge and awareness of cultural differences. My hope is that through this essay I can provide a bridge for thinking about pedagogy not only for our Native American students, but for other diverse peoples as well.

My question is how pedagogy in theological education that is generally constructed on a Western European model could be reconstructed so that it is more hospitable to receiving the deep richness of the diverse cultures in our midst. We need to include pedagogy that draws on what is learned through experience in community by beginning with connectedness and

Proleptic Pedagogy

vision, in addition to the convictions passed on to us through our denominational traditions and analytical thinking. *My thesis is that we need to be intentional in developing pedagogy that is inclusive of the ways that persons from diverse races and cultures learn, including support of divergent thinking.* I will develop the issues raised in this classroom incident as they relate to Native Americans based on my teaching experience and the 2009 research project, but will later draw implications for creating pedagogy that is hospitable to other diverse peoples and divergent thinkers in our midst.

*Worldview and Social Location*

In many ways, finding commonality with Native American cultures compared to African American and Hispanic cultures is even more difficult because Native American and Western European worldviews are so different that it is almost impossible to find a bridge. The classroom incident begins to reveal the radical difference in worldviews between Western European and Native American thinkers. Jace Weaver in his discussion of Native American religious education goes so far as to say that it is almost impossible to bridge this divide: "To speak of religious education and Native Americans is to engage in a kind of incommensurate discourse. The Western European-American worldview common to most religious educators is quite different from the Native worldview. This incommensurability and the near impossibility of translating from one thought world to the other complicate the task of religious education."[3] In other words, the conceptual framework and expression of the two worldviews have little or no connection. To emphasize his point, Weaver uses a story from Vine Deloria to elaborate: "An old Indian man's saying captures the radical difference between Indian and Western peoples quite adequately. The white man, the Indians maintain, has ideas; Indians have visions. Ideas have a single dimension and require a chain of connected ideas to make sense. . . . The vision, on the other hand, presents a whole picture of experience and has a central meaning that stands on its own feet as an independent revelation."[4] There are those who would read Deloria's words and immediately argue that "white men" also have visions, indicating that they do not understand or respect the magnitude of the difference here. In fact, it would not be uncommon for some to easily co-opt, and thereby dismiss Deloria's idea

3. Weaver, "Native Americans and Religious Education," 267–68.
4. Ibid.

by amending his words to read "Christians have a vision that presents a whole picture of experience and has a central meaning that stands on its own feet as an independent revelation." Not only is this wrong-headed and wrong-hearted, but it prevents us from hearing what Deloria meant. If we are going to explore issues of pedagogy for diverse peoples with integrity, we need to recognize the difference in our social locations and bracket our own experience and assumptions. We need to see what truth there is for us in Deloria's words as we wrestle with pedagogy for diverse peoples in theological education.

For the purposes of this discussion, I am going to begin by identifying Deloria's distinctions as the "rational" contrasted with the "relational" approach. This is an admittedly reductionist view, but it is a place to start. While rational explanations do provide meaning for our lives, what is lost by exclusive use of this approach is a holistic view of the world as rich with possibilities and untold meanings. A rational method also carries an implicit assumption that Euro-Americans have the power of language to name and explain for everyone rather than looking into the heart, mind, and social location of those who are different from us in order to listen and to learn. What is central in the relational approach of Native American cultures is the experiential connection to all of life. What stands behind their vision is a worldview that has no need to explain everything. It just is. Dr. Martin Brokenleg calls this "heart thinking," a perspective shaped by "symbol, ceremony, repetition, impressionism, and concrete discreet concepts" that leave much unexplained.[5] In other words, meaning is more visual and symbolic than literate. The more intuitive perspective of the heart maintains an element of mystery, of something or someone(s) larger than the whole, of answers and reasons beyond our knowledge or comprehension.

Our Christian traditions teach that there is a God who is larger than all of creation, but many of our interpretations and understandings are more "rational" than "relational," as we focus on preaching the Word and primarily using words to articulate our faith. In many of our communities, we strive to recover the experience and feeling of being part of a larger community with shared beliefs, values, and practices. Brokenleg contrasts these two perspectives in his depiction of the "cataphatic thought" of the West that "defines and explains what is known or understood" and the Native American cultural pattern of "apophatic thought [that] prefers not to

---

5. Martin Brokenleg, "Native American Cultural Patterns" PowerPoint and Lecture. University of Kansas Medical School, November 30, 2009. Used by permission.

define nor to explain, [and] leaves much unstated."⁶ In this interpretation, Brokenleg lifts up a comparison between analytical and global thinking, which hold different perceptions of time and space. While this proposal does bring clarity about the contrast between religion as a system of belief based more on analytical thinking and religion as a way of life seen through the eyes of relational thinking, it should be noted that there are groups and denominations within Christianity that emphasize a more experiential perspective on faith.

The critical distinction in these two ways of life and faith seems to come in terms of an emphasis on "individual" experiences of transformation in Christian communities contrasted with an emphasis on communal identity and shared experience in the Native communities. Weaver describes the distinction that Western traditions are characterized by focus on belief using "linear thinking" and "chronological perception" while Native American cultures focus on ritual and way of communal life using "global thinking" and "spatial perception."⁷ Weaver's distinctions combined with the ideas from Brokenleg give us insight into Rev. Moss's dilemma with theological education and emphasize the need for us to create pedagogy that is inclusive of both global and analytical learners and their different perspectives on time and space.

The hidden possibility in creating pedagogy for theological education that attends to both analytical and global thinking is that students and faculty could learn from each other using these approaches. In research on Carol Gilligan's original theory comparing Kohlberg's "ethic of justice," to her own proposal for an "ethic of response and care," Gilligan articulated the contrast between those who primarily see themselves as "separated and objective" in "relationships of reciprocity" and those who see themselves as "connected" in "relationships of response."⁸ The group identified as separated knowers are most concerned with the rules of the game and fair play, while the connected knowers will choose care for relationships over following the rules. I have found it helpful to talk with students about identifying their primary orientation as analytical or separated thinkers or global or connected thinkers. The separated thinkers are those who can easily separate out a small part of an issue or idea for critical analysis. The connected

---

6. Brokenleg, "Native American Cultural Patterns," Power Point, slide 31. Used by permission.

7. Weaver, "Native Americans and Religious Education," 268–70.

8. Gilligan, et al.,. *Mapping the Moral Domain*, 35.

thinkers in our classrooms are those who have to look at the big picture in order to consider the connections between the parts. It just doesn't seem right or possible for them to consider one part of an issue without considering the consequences for the whole.

All of our students who are preparing to provide leadership for the church need to develop their skills in both analytical and global thinking, and Gilligan's researchers indicate that this is possible. D. Kay Johnston used two of Aesop's fables to assess moral orientation in sixth graders.[9] Both orientations, ethics of justice focused on rights (separated) and ethics of care focused on response (connected) were used by the students in some way, but they went first to the orientation that was most comfortable to them in solving a moral dilemma. What was striking, however, was that by age eleven, all of the students could switch to the other perspective when asked "Is there another way to solve the problem?"[10] Even more telling was the fact that "the girls as a group choose both orientations more frequently than the boys who tend as a group to use the rights orientation more exclusively" even though they are aware of the response orientation.[11] These research results make an even stronger case for rethinking our pedagogy in theological education to incorporate both analytical (mind) and global (heart) thinking into our teaching and learning so that theological education becomes more hospitable and engaging to students from diverse cultures, and more holistic for all. This would also provide an opportunity for all of our students to develop their skills in using these different perspectives in connection to their cultural identity and social location.

## Identity and Community

While we could find connections for all of our students by incorporating analytical and global thinking into our pedagogy and assessment, this is only a beginning in helping us understand the difference between Native cultures and Eurocentric cultures. Another significant difference is found in the values that shape identity in the Native American cultures: tribal identification through a network of extended family relationships, collaboration, respect for others and creation, and responsibility for the community. Identity begins in living with a community where stories about all of life

---

9. Johnston, "Adolescents' Solutions to Dilemmas," 60.
10. Ibid.
11. Ibid., 60–61.

shape identity and way of life. A sample from Paula Gunn Allen's account of her mother's Laguna Pueblo stories helps us understand the power of story in shaping identity in the midst of community:

> My mother told me stories about cooking and childbearing; . . . about the land and the sky, . . . she told me stories about going to dances and getting married; . . . stories about herself, her mother, about her grandmother . . . She told me stories about living and dying. And in all those stories, she told me who I was, who I was supposed to be, whom I came from, and who would follow me. In this way she taught me the meaning of the words she said, that all life is a circle and everything has a place within it.[12]

Allen's description points to identity as participation in a community's way of life framed in story. In other words, identity is shaped in community with strong connections to family, faith, and cultural traditions for Native Americans and this would also be true of other diverse peoples such as African Americans, Hispanics, and Latinos/Latinas. This value of community is often evident in introductions that begin with relationships to family and ancestry, not with individual achievements.

Identity from a Western European perspective draws on values of individuality, independence, autonomy, expectations of increasing differentiation and competency in skills and abilities over time, self-determination, and personal achievement. We might experience community in social groups or in the church, but that is probably not our primary identification. We are known for who we are and what we accomplish as individuals. Our introductions often begin with our names and what we do and what we have accomplished. In many of the developmental theories developed in the 60s, a sign of maturity was this ability to know ourselves as distinct from others. In these theories, developmental issues must be addressed in each stage of life as one matures, always arising in the same order regardless of gender or culture. In more recent years, Christian educators have countered the idea that the task of Christian formation was to focus on helping individuals move through these stages with proposals that address shared faith journeys within faith communities. Brett Webb-Mitchell has focused his work on pilgrimage: "Pilgrimage connotes a movement, a journeying toward the telos of God's dominion: a beginning, middle, and end, in which we 'grow up in every way in him who is the head, into Christ, from whom the whole body' of Christ

---

12. Allen, *Sacred Hoop*, 46.

## Pedagogical Issues in Theological Education

is 'knitted together in love'" (Eph. 4:15–16).[13] For Webb-Mitchell, growth in faith is a journey in relationship with God toward a vision of being joined with the body of Christ in God's love. Another proposal comes from Maria Harris who sees persons growing in terms of wholeness through practicing spiritual disciplines, study of the Christian tradition, and service in a movement toward the telos of "communion of all."[14] My own work in Christian faith formation in the Wesleyan tradition has taken the idea of growing in communion with God through a shared focus on what God does and what we do. This process of Christian faith formation is located in the congregation as a community of grace. The emphasis in this proposal is that God is the one who first invites us into communion and who continues to guide us in developing communion and finally full communion with God.[15] In these educational theories, a move back toward seeing our faith as a way of life within community rather than a series of stages that must be completed at a normative age is evident. Identity is formed in a community of faith through a shared journey toward the reign of God. While not completing the bridge between the global and communal orientation of Native Americans and other diverse peoples, it is a beginning.

### Divergent Thinking

A related issue evident in this discussion is the not so implicit consequence that much of theological curriculum in traditional seminary education in the United States focuses on knowledge of the Christian tradition (linear thinking in chronological time) with only limited time to explore creative options for ministry and leadership (global thinking and spatial perception). Some of the more "traditional" seminaries focus on knowledge and rely on learning how to apply it in the practice of ministry after graduation. Our history at Saint Paul School of Theology has been to focus on the integration of theory and practice by creating opportunities within our classes to bring examples from ministry into discussion and/or to create designs for ministry using the content of the course. While knowledge and understanding of the tradition of the church is critically important, it needs to be brought into relationship with the practice of ministry in all of its diverse forms. This praxis model of theological education recognizes that the

13. Webb-Mitchell, "Leaving Development Behind," 149.
14. Harris and Moran, "Educating Persons," 70.
15. Matthaei, *Formation in Faith*.

content of theological education informs and shapes practice of ministry. In turn, questions raised in the practice of ministry shape our understanding of the content of theological education, and the whole process provides a space for the creativity of diverse thinking. But even this praxis model would be more hospitable to diverse peoples and divergent thinkers by more attention to and acceptance of global thinking and spatial perception characteristic of divergent thinkers.

Divergent thinkers see many possible answers to a question, find value in all of them, and can use their critical reflection skills to sort and define the most promising choices. We would call them "creative thinkers." Sir Ken Robinson in an RSA video for public education, "Changing Educational Paradigms," demonstrates how the Enlightenment thinking still dominates education and argues that we should leave "conveyor belt" education behind because it takes everyone through the same process based on age group.[16] Robinson is arguing that in this approach intelligence is defined as deductive reasoning and allows little room for inductive reasoning that would be more helpful for many theological students, including those from diverse cultures. Of note in this video is mention of a longitudinal research project reported in the book, *Break Point and Beyond*, documenting that 98% of kindergartners score at genius level in divergent thinking. The percentage decreases to 50% by ten years and to 25% by fifteen years as children become more "educated."[17] Robinson concludes that the problem with the Enlightenment approach is that "we are trying to address the future by what we have done in the past."[18] The question that Robinson raises for pedagogy in theological education is, "How do persons maintain their cultural and religious identity while engaging the global community in this new age of ministry?" Robinson's YouTube video presents a provocative and entertaining argument about the loss of creative thinking and challenges us to reflect on how recovering divergent thinking could transform theological education and re-create the expressions of church for our time. As Robinson notes, this loss of creative thinking is also exacerbated by the loss of the arts in education since it is our aesthetic imagination that nurtures creativity. The use of arts in theological education is particularly important since the arts could help us creatively address the needs of the church and the shape of theological education for the future in the midst of increasing

16. Robinson, "Changing Educational Paradigms" RSA, 6:56.
17. Ibid., 8:43.
18. Ibid., 1:04.

diversity. Considering knowledge and proposals for the practice of ministry through divergent thinking would expand our imaginations about new forms of ministries that will renew the church in this contemporary world.

## Engaging Pedagogical Literature

Our Wabash grant on "proleptic pedagogy" provided a variety of resources and workshops related to learning and racial/ethnic diversity in theological education. How educational environments reflect the cultural expectations and practices of the educators was emphasized in the work of Alicia Fedelina Chávez and Florence Guido-DiBrito:

> It is critical to understand the culturally constructed nature of educational environments and to develop an awareness of the effect of our own racially and ethnically defined sense of self, of learning, and of education. Difficulties arise for many minority and international adult learners when they attempt to negotiate learning environments that have been constructed within an ethnic base of values, behaviors, beliefs, and ways of doing things that is different from their own. Unfortunately, these racial and ethnic manifestations in the learning process are usually unconsciously applied by educators and peers, making them difficult to identify, examine, and modify.[19]

It is obvious from the authors' words that one of the greatest challenges we face in developing pedagogy for diverse persons and divergent thinkers is how to increase our awareness of the implicit values, behaviors, and expectations embedded in our teaching. It is our lack of awareness that results in students from diverse racial and ethnic backgrounds feeling homesick, stupid, and displaced in our seminaries. We could see it in Rev. Moss's words, "I felt like the way I understood things to be was invalid and had no significance." If our aim is to develop the gifts of all students, we need to be intentional in finding ways to uncover these hidden elements in our teaching. The words of Frank Tuitt challenge us: "It is not enough to help students learn to read and write in traditional classrooms without challenging assumptions, paradigms, and hegemonic characteristics embedded in the learning process."[20] In other words, we need to find ways to

---

19. Chávez and Guido-DeBrito, "Racial and Ethnic Identity and Development," 44.
20. Tuitt, "Realizing a More Inclusive Pedagogy," 246.

become more self-aware about how our values, behaviors, and expectations are culture bound.

## Culturally Hospitable Pedagogy

The injustice in our current theological pedagogy was highlighted in Rev. Moss' discussion of an educational process that privileges analytical thinking and often does not provide a forum for sharing the rich experience and relational connections of our students. Kathleen Talvacchia addresses this issue when she argues that "we can more effectively teach in ways that promote social justice when we begin to understand experiences of marginalization that are the lived reality of groups other than ourselves. Also we can understand our own experiences of marginalization or privilege in relation to the experience of others. This involves developing a multicultural sensitivity that is a habit of mind and heart rather than a form of political correctness."[21] Talvacchia challenges us to imagine what it means to stand in the shoes of those who are different from ourselves, to learn about the lives and experiences of our students, and to rethink pedagogy in light of our new awareness. In other words, what I call *culturally hospitable pedagogy* needs to be about fairness so that all students are provided equal access to a learning process that connects with their cultural experience.

We need to be intentional in developing pedagogy rooted in deep knowledge of the diverse communities from which our students come, a pedagogy that is inclusive of the ways that persons from diverse races and cultures learn and supports divergent thinking. In my research for this grant, I found an important insight when Tuitt cited Knelfelkamp in their research on pedagogy in diverse classrooms:

> According to Knefelkamp, the challenge of educating racially diverse students is no different from the very same challenges that an increasingly racially diverse society generates for this country. How can educators create classrooms in which all students, regardless of racial background, have a chance to succeed? If we can't succeed in the classroom, what hope do we have for the larger society? Inclusive pedagogy offers professors some guidance as to how they might reconsider their teaching practices in light of these challenges.[22]

21. Talvacchia, *Critical Minds and Discerning Hearts*, 4.
22. Tuitt, "Realizing a More Inclusive Pedagogy," 258.

Here Knefelkamp is pointing out the connection between educating racially diverse students and the reality of U.S. society, most graphically seen in the crowd waiting for President Obama to speak on election night in Chicago. That picture is burned into my mind as who we, the people of the United States, are today. So I would ask Knefelkamp's question in the context of seminary preparation for leaders in the church: "If we can't succeed in educating racially and culturally diverse students in the classroom, what hope is there for the future of the church?"

Creating an inclusive pedagogy in theological education requires an intense commitment on the part of the whole learning community to see what is unseen in our pedagogy and community life, in the ways we teach and the ways we live together in our common enterprise. Tuitt offers the following characteristics of an inclusive pedagogy:

1. "Faculty-student interaction"—faculty interest in and availability to students in informal social settings is essential for "students who need to feel connected to the group, who are aware of being upset when their own voices are not heard, and who do not believe that the instructor is the sole source of knowledge (Zimmerman, 1991)."

2. "Sharing Power"—professors and students work together in exploring ideas and everyone is responsible for contributing; faculty—power of grading; recognizing one's own limits of knowledge.

3. "Dialogical professor-student interaction—values student voices as much as faculty expertise."

4. "Activation of student voice"—provide opportunities for self-expression through journals, chat groups on course management software, small group discussion before full group discussion, awareness of context and cultural practices.

5. "Utilization of personal narratives"—making connections between ideas and students' life experience."[23]

This list of characteristics demonstrates the challenge and magnitude of the task, but also generates excitement about how to create theological pedagogy that is hospitable to all of our students.

---

23. Ibid., 247–50.

Proleptic Pedagogy

*Pedagogy and Spirituality*

Because we are thinking about teaching in theological education, it is impossible to consider pedagogy without discussing its connection to spirituality. Elizabeth Tisdell's work in *Exploring Spirituality and Culture in Adult and Higher Education* addresses how spirituality shapes the way we teach, implicitly and usually unconsciously.[24] If we think about it, we know Tisdell's observation is true. As faithful persons, our teaching ministry reflects our faith, and recognizing how this happens contributes to developing a pedagogy that is hospitable to diverse persons and divergent thinkers. And other assumptions about spirituality that Tisdell named have been evident throughout this essay in that spirituality involves the interconnectedness of all creation, provides meaning for our lives, and awakens self-awareness that it is part of our authenticity and clarity in teaching.[25] From a different perspective, Talvacchia writes, "The spirituality of multicultural teaching encompasses a deep and abiding concern for understanding identity groups in their social location of difference and teaching in a manner that honors that difference. It is a vocational commitment to teach what must be taught in a manner that makes it accessible to all persons, so that the power of knowledge can be for all groups in society and not just members of the dominant culture."[26] Talvacchia is discussing the connection between spirituality and justice in that our concern for knowing and understanding our students promotes fairness in the classroom.

    We can emphasize the connection between pedagogy and spirituality in our thinking and planning using a variety of teaching and learning activities. Tisdell writes, "Spirituality is about how people construct knowledge through largely unconscious and symbolic processes, often made more concrete in art forms such as music, image, symbol, and ritual, all of which are manifested culturally."[27] Here Tisdell is pointing us toward a pedagogy that is not only rooted in spirituality, but includes a variety of forms for helping our students construct knowledge for leadership in the church. I am including an abridged list of her ideas for "spiritually grounded and culturally relevant pedagogy" here in the hope that it will help us think about how to construct a hospitable pedagogy for our teaching:

24. Tisdell, *Exploring Spirituality and Culture*, ix.
25. Ibid., xi.
26. Talvacchia, *Critical Minds and Discerning Hearts*, 23.
27. Tisdell, *Exploring Spirituality and Culture*, xi.

- An emphasis on authenticity (both spiritual and cultural)
- An environment that allows for the exploration of the cognitive, affective and relational, and symbolic
- Readings that reflect the cultures of the members of the class, and the cultural pluralism of the geographical area relevant to course content
- Exploration of individual and communal dimensions of cultural and other dimensions of identity
- Collaborative work that envisions and presents manifestations of multiple dimensions of learning and strategies for change
- Celebration of learning and provision for closure to the course
- Recognition of the limitations of the higher education classroom, and that transformation in an ongoing process that takes time.[28]

In my experience of being intentional about using Tisdell's ideas in the spiritual direction class, I discovered why she has named them. The whole tenor of the class was different. All students, including Rev. Moss, found a way to engage in the course and to share the gifts that they brought to our enthusiastic and substantive discussion from their diverse racial and ethnic backgrounds.

## Considering a Theology of Pedagogy

My motivation to create hospitable pedagogy has come from a lifetime of working with a variety of persons in the church. The transition to seminary teaching happened quickly, but it took about five years for me to grow into my identity as teacher, and I continue to learn more about myself and teaching today as I near retirement. It is always a work in progress. When I first started teaching at Saint Paul, I wore a blazer every day and I had a candle in the classroom. The blazer helped me take on the responsibility and authority of teaching as I made the transition from graduate student to teacher in three months. The candle reminded me that God is the teacher and what God expects of me is that I will offer myself and my knowledge and skills to my best ability and trust that God will use what I offer in others' lives. It was great comfort to me as a new teacher to remember that I did not have to have all the answers, but could accompany students on their journeys to find the answers that they sought through shared critical

28. Ibid., 212–13.

reflection. To this day, I continue to have a candle in the classroom. Over time, I have come to understand that learning is an act of worship because we are developing the gifts that God has given us for our Christian vocations. So the candle designates sacred space that calls us to treat each other with respect and to listen to each other with our hearts. Now each class also begins with music, reflection and/or prayer and ends with a closing thought for our sending out. These brief rituals provide great opportunity to bring in resources from diverse cultures and religious traditions, including offerings by students. The belief that God is at work in the teaching and learning process raises awareness that we learn from each other. And this awareness is critically important in creating an environment that is hospitable to diverse peoples and divergent thinkers.

The theology behind this understanding is my belief that God calls us to love all of creation, including our human neighbors. The great commandment teaches us to love God and neighbor (Mt. 22:36–40). And in my Wesleyan tradition, when John Wesley was asked, "Who is my neighbor?" his reply was, "Every [person] in the world; every child of [God]."[29] In other words, Wesley made it very clear that *every* person is our neighbor, even those we would not chose for ourselves. It's a challenging concept, but when we open our lives and hearts to hear the stories of those who are different from ourselves, we receive new awareness of who God is and how God works in people's lives that we would have missed otherwise. And it is in our relationships with others that we discover ourselves. As Parker Palmer writes, "Self is a moving intersection of many other selves. We are formed by the lives which intersect with ours. The larger and richer our community, the larger and richer is the content of the self."[30] If we take Palmer's words seriously, then we realize that our lives can be enriched by our relationships with all members of our seminary community through hospitable pedagogy in theological education.

## Constructing a Pedagogical Proposal

This reflection on pedagogical issues for diverse peoples and divergent thinkers in theological education has highlighted my commitment and passion for creating a pedagogy that is hospitable to all students by being attentive to race, culture, and just practices in the classroom. In this

29. Wesley, "The Almost Christian," 137.
30. Palmer, *Promise of Paradox*, 74.

*Pedagogical Issues in Theological Education*

proposal, I begin with institutional commitment needed to create pedagogy for diverse peoples and divergent thinkers and end with a brief discussion of insights from my research for this chapter. I originally developed this proposal out of my Wabash research project on the history, culture, and values of Native peoples in order to provide a culturally relevant pedagogy for Native American students, but the process applies to any racial/ethnic group a seminary might want to address.

1. *Immersion in Native Cultures*: Commitment to a year-long study of and engagement with Native cultures by all elements of the seminary community including students, staff, faculty, administration, trustees, and graduate council. Some elements of this immersion could include a) gaining familiarity with the history of the attempt, including the church's participation, to destroy Native peoples and their cultures; b) listening to stories of the elders in the Oklahoma Indian Missionary Conference; and c) immersions designed by the Oklahoma Indian Missionary Conference—weekend, week-long, month-long that would involve listening, study, working, sharing together

2. *Professional Development for Faculty*: The primary learning from my research is that we need intention and resources for professional development of faculty. The most helpful document that provided a beginning point for my own thinking about culturally hospitable pedagogy was "Diversity within Unity: Essential principles for Teaching and Learning in a Multicultural Society,"[31] and I would recommend it for all faculty, particularly since it applies to all racial and ethnic groups. Create a time to study and construct a culturally hospitable pedagogy by a) bringing in a Native American consultant to share experience and knowledge about Native American students in higher education in relation to pedagogy; b) consultation and collaboration among faculty members about how knowledge and experience of these cultures contribute to developing pedagogy; and c) creating and critiquing course construction and teaching plans in a collegial environment focused on hospitable pedagogy.

3. *Spiritual and Financial Support for Native American Students*: A literature review notes that student support is critical for a hospitable pedagogy. Some areas of support include a) preparation for teaching by reviewing research about Native American students, how they learn

---

31. Banks, et al., "Diversity within Unity."

and why they fail; b) providing informal gathering times with one or more faculty members and Native American students for discussion and sharing; c) offering support for developing academic work such as writing workshops and peer tutors; d) providing computers so students can participate in hybrid courses from their homes; and e) raising endowment for financial aid to provide scholarships.

4. *Institutional Support:* Additional actions by a seminary committed to creating a hospitable cultural environment for Native American students would include a) hiring additional Native American faculty, adjuncts, and contextual education leaders; and b) developing a capital campaign to provide faculty, staff, financial aid, technology.

If our aim in theological education is to prepare leaders to renew the church and to transform the world, then we must consider the challenges of creating a culturally hospitable pedagogy. Through this discussion, four primary proposals have emerged:

*Embrace Pedagogical Development*

We can no longer base pedagogy in theological education solely on a western European model with its inherent values, behaviors, and expectations. To enrich our educational environment, we need to engage diverse peoples and divergent thinkers, both faculty and students, in creating pedagogies for our new reality—a more culturally diverse country in a global community. Engaging diverse perspectives will help us think about the shape and role of the church in a global society, particularly in the changing cultural demographics in United States culture.

*Embrace the Use of the Arts*

Arts hold the promise of generating creativity in thinking about and imagining a new vision for the church. Not only do the arts help diverse peoples give expression to theological meaning, but also they connect with our souls and provide access to the heart of our spirituality. The arts challenge us to help us think beyond what we know and add depth to pedagogy by leading us to think with our hearts, as well as our minds.

## Embrace Collaborative Learning

Options for collaborative learning alongside individual learning are critical for a culturally hospitable pedagogy. Collaboration enhances learning as students work together with their teachers and each other to integrate knowledge and the practice of ministry. This not only offers students an opportunity to work from their strengths, but the shared ideas and imagination will lead to deeper community and sustained learning.

My most recent conversation with Rev. Moss was about vision. Vision is related to heart thinking, and she talked with great passion about being captured by a vision that guides her. How this happens cannot be explained, but Rev. Moss emphasizes that it is important to share the vision because it is not an individual gift, so communal sharing and thinking is important. As Rev. Moss and I talked, I realized that my vision for a culturally hospitable pedagogy was being enriched and stretched beyond what I could imagine on my own. And this is the gift of a commitment to loving God and our neighbors so much that we seek to understand their lives and longings in order to construct a pedagogy that creates space for the sharing of their gifts as we learn together.

# 8

# Hip-Hop in the Classroom

F. Douglas Powe Jr.

### Telling a Classroom Story

I TEACH A CLASS AT Saint Paul School of Theology entitled, "The African American Church in Postmodernity" that seeks to help students think about renewing African American congregations through engaging hip-hop. In the second class session on September 11, 2012, I began with a YouTube clip of Jay-Z and Kanye West's "No Church in the Wild."[1] The students' reading for the week was focused on the meaning of postmodernity and particularly African American perspectives on postmodernity. My expectation was that students would be able to take what they read from the texts and analyze the lyrics projected on the screen.

The inability of many students to exegete the hip-hop lyrics based upon what they read surprised me. These were not first year students who had no clue how to do integrative work or how to do basic exegesis. While thinking about postmodernity from an African American perspective was probably new, the topic of postmodernity was not new. What was new to the students was thinking theologically about hip-hop. Using hip-hop as a

---

1. Jay-Z and Kanye West, "No Church in the Wild."

resource for deepening their understanding of postmodernity threw many of the students for a loop.

One of the questions I continuously ponder is, "Are seminaries adequately preparing students to be cultural exegetes?" The importance of this question is whether or not seminarians are able to do integrative work that moves beyond typical theory and praxis models. I define integrative work in this adaptation from a syllabus from a team-taught class as

> [The] challenge clergy face in trying to balance creativity and discipline while synthesizing the issues and needs of their communities and congregations by maintaining theological, scriptural, and ethical integrity. Consequently the course emphasizes interdisciplinary and theological methods in service of the church and her ministries. The nature of the course prepares students for this integrative task of ministry by using theology, hip-hop and exemplars to model holistic reflection. The course invites students to reflect on African American ecclesial renewal by developing their own theological positions in response to challenging conversations with hip-hop artists and hip-hop theologians.[2]

In other words, the course is designed to better prepare students for being cultural exegetes utilizing hip-hop as its lens.

## Identifying the Pedagogical Challenges

The pedagogical challenges in recognizing hip-hop as a theological resource include acknowledging one's own experience without privileging it, not allowing students simply to dismiss hip-hop resources, and appropriately structuring the class. My goal is to develop students who are excellent cultural exegetes even if their ministry setting is not in an African American context. This requires addressing pedagogical issues related to teaching, learning and integrative thinking. In this chapter, *I am arguing that utilizing hip-hop as a resource re-frames the way that students will consider and use theological material in their ministry contexts.* This essay is a first effort to outline some of the ways in which utilizing hip-hop resources can impact a deeper understanding of racial and ethnic diversity in theological pedagogy.

---

2. This statement was adapted from the Howell and Powe syllabus for APS 430 Advanced Praxis Seminar: Theology in Black and White at Saint Paul School of Theology, Fall 2011.

Proleptic Pedagogy

The primary challenge in this instance is in helping students to apply their exegetical and integrative thinking skills in a different way. Most students take "The African American Church in Postmodernity" in the middle or near the end of their studies. The expectation is that students have some background in Bible, systematic theology, and contextual education. This course builds on the skills learned in those disciplines by helping students to think more deeply about confronting the decline in African American congregations. An "excellent student" is one who at the end of the semester can use interdisciplinary thinking continuously to exegete culture for the purpose of African American ecclesial renewal.

One of the pedagogical challenges in cultivating excellence in our students requires the acknowledgment of the diverse backgrounds and experiences of students without privileging either. The students who enroll in the class are African American, Anglo American and Korean. Typically there is gender and age diversity. Given the narrow way in which I define the class and the variety of experiences that the students bring, one of the pedagogical challenges is to help students engage hip-hop as a culture different than their own in doing integrative work.[3] The tendency is for students either to think hip-hop operates like their favorite genre of music or to dismiss completely hip-hop altogether. Developing pedagogical strategies that help students escape the snares of either extreme is important for the success of the class.

An important pedagogical strategy that helps navigate the extremes of blind favoritism or dismissal is listening. The ability to listen to the hip-hop artists and engage them with critical theological ears is the goal. The ability for students to do this form of listening requires not getting stuck in their personal experiences and being open to others. Emilie Townes describes it this way: "What we must be about as we approach one another's work is care-filled listening and observing and engagement."[4] Townes is challenging those outside of her African American context, particularly Anglo American women, not to move so quickly to add one's voice. Townes articulates the pedagogical approach I seek to model in helping students to engage hip-hop resources.

Another pedagogical challenge is helping students realize that hip-hop resources have theological value. A legitimate concern with hip-hop is misogyny and violence. Some dismiss hip-hop as perpetuating all that is bad or

---

3. Engaging a culture different than their own also applies to many of the African American students who perceive hip-hop as something outside of the church.

4. Townes, "Appropriation and Reciprocity," 116.

problematic with society. This attitude is enhanced when hip-hop is perceived as the opposite of appropriate ecclesial concerns. I have to engage students in such a way that does not deny the issues related to hip-hop, but at the same time challenges them to think about the theological value of hip-hop.

The pedagogical strategy for assisting students to do this is raising awareness of the importance of naming, allowing those in the hip-hop community to name their reality even when we find it difficult to deal with the way in which they name it. Townes speaks to this issue from the perspective of a womanist, but I believe it is applicable for my class. She states, "Take care when you name my reality."[5] Her point is that womanists during the late eighties and early nineties were still figuring out their own reality, and they did not want others to jump in to name their reality for them. We can learn from Townes and apply this strategy to hip-hop resources by listening carefully rather than making judgments and naming the artists' reality for them. In no way should we water down our critiques of misogyny and violence, but we should not carelessly name that reality without first listening for the deeper meaning.

Finally, developing an appropriate structure for the class in terms of bringing in hip-hop resources is a significant pedagogical challenge. It would be easy to make hip-hop simply an add on and not an integral part of the class. For example, students could engage a few hip-hop resources, but not engage the real work of diving into the theological texts. If I allow this approach to become the structure of the class, then I am simply perpetuating pedagogical strategies that I am hoping to counter.

A better approach is to make the hip-hop resources primary. This means structuring the class in such a way that those resources are engaged in the same way as other materials so that deep integration is possible. One way I accomplish this pedagogically is to start every class with a hip-hop resource that relates to the theological theme of the week and to spend half of the class time engaging that particular resource. This will ensure students are steeped in the hip-hop resources as well as other theological resources.

## Engaging Pedagogical Literature

The student learning outcome for this class is that "[s]tudents will make imaginative proposals for renewing African American congregations drawing

---

5. Ibid., 117.

upon critical engagement with hip-hop culture."[6] The evidence to illustrate students can do this is an ability to do integrative work that speaks to their context. At a minimum, three things need to occur to help students achieve the learning outcome in a way that demonstrates integrative thinking.

First, students must learn to name the cognitive dissonance they often experience when encountering hip-hop culture.[7] In class this cognitive dissonance typically shows up related to language, comprehension of lyrics, and dis-ease with hip-hop attire. For example, listening to Meek Mill's rap "Amen" and hearing him seemingly disparage the church can be challenging for students. The cognitive dissonance often occurs when something from hip-hop culture challenges students' current worldview.

In our Wabash grant resource, Kathleen Talvacchia describes an experience in Brazil where she and other students experienced dis-ease with hearing a Brazilian woman supporting prostitution.[8] She finally realizes that it is her own cognitive dissonance with what is "inherently immoral" that is not allowing her to fully engage the Brazilian woman.[9] Talvaccia's insight in Brazil helps us to understand the struggle for many students with a hip-hop culture that often uses profanity in lyrics, interviews and just everyday conversation. The use of profanity creates a cognitive dissonance for some students who perceive it as antithetical to church culture.

It is not only the use of profanity that deters some students; it is also the misogynistic images, lyrics, etc. that many find over the top. One example is the relationship between Biggie Smalls and Lil Kim that is portrayed in the story of his life—*Notorious*. Many students see this portrayal and hear the lyrics to "Get Money" and understandably experience a cognitive dissonance with the reality that is being expressed. Returning to Talvacchia's struggles to fully engage another context in Brazil,[10] it is often hard for students to make the shift that what they hear in rap lyrics is a lived reality by some (e.g., Biggie and Lil Kim).

It is not only language that causes a cognitive dissonance for many students it is also seeking to comprehend the raps and lyrics. For many students,

6. Powe, Syllabus for CHS 340 African American Church in Postmodernity, Fall 2012.

7. Cannon, *Katie's Canon*, 139. Cannon talks about this in terms of students' "belief systems, lifestyles," etc., but my focus is more directly related to hip-hop culture.

8. Talvacchia, *Critical Minds and Discerning Hearts*, 20.

9. Ibid.

10. Ibid.

## Hip-Hop in the Classroom

the rap artists speak too quickly, and the students cannot follow what is being said in its entirety. Many of these students also struggle comprehending the lyrics even when they are reading them in written form. For many it is almost like decoding a language that is somewhat familiar, but at the same time foreign.

Finally, the attire within hip-hop culture is perceived as problematic. Ralph Watkins names this issue for the Civil Rights Generation when he writes, "The civil rights generation fought to open doors and break down barriers to ensure the next generations' success. When the civil rights generation sees pants hanging down, hears speakers bumping in cars, and notices girls with thongs rising out of the back of their pants, they look in disgust."[11] Certainly it is not only the Civil Rights Generation that responds this way to hip-hop culture when it comes to attire.

For students to achieve the learning outcome I desire, it is important for them to name the cognitive dissonance related to language, comprehension and hip-hop attire. Naming the ways in which these issues inhibit them from critically engaging the material opens up a space for dialogue that helps many students to return to the hip-hop resources with an epistemological nuance. Many students do not agree with the profane language or attire, but are able to engage the hip-hop resources critically because they have an understanding of what causes the cognitive dissonance. Talvacchia describes this moment in her dialogue with the Brazilian woman: "I was doing to the speaker what had been done to me."[12] She means by this pre-judging based upon her sexual orientation.[13] This is often the way in which we pre-judge hip-hop culture that causes a cognitive dissonance.

Another way for students to achieve the desired learning goal is listening with new ears and seeing with new eyes to develop an understanding of the push back to African American congregations. I started this essay with the example of Jay-Z and Kanya West's collaboration "No Church in the Wild." The challenge the students encountered the first time they watched the video is only catching a fourth of the lyrics, and the video itself seemed disconnected. The students were working with unfamiliar resources. The ability to listen deeply to what these artists were saying, to take it in visually by watching the video, and to delve into the lyrics assists students in forming new ears and eyes for understanding. Developing these new ways of seeing

11. Watkins, *Gospel Remix*, 12.
12. Ibid.
13. Ibid.

Proleptic Pedagogy

and listening requires continuously working with and engaging hip-hop resources. It requires watching and reading things a few times before they make sense. In the case of "No Church in the Wild," many students worked with the resources for a week before things started to make sense. The good news is as the semester continued, things started to make sense sooner.

I perceive this listening and seeing in new ways as a process of conscientizing. Students are being made aware of a different way in which to engage the culture and particularly African American church culture. This conscientizing process requires moving out of one's comfort zone and a willingness to engage critically that which is unfamiliar. Kathleen Talvacchia explains it in this manner: "Listening demands attentiveness to another, an active participation in what that person is revealing. But the goal of listening is not only hearing, but understanding. We listen so that we may know more fully and completely. We cannot understand if we do not listen. At the same time, increased understanding allows us to listen with greater sensitivity and comprehension. When we listen deeply, we can begin to comprehend another."[14] Talvacchia helps us to understand how listening is a method of critical engagement with another that truly puts us in dialogue with the other. The benefit for students in my class is they start to engage critically African American culture enabling to them to dialogue with it in new ways.

It is also my hope that students achieve the desired learning goal by becoming good cultural exegetes. I consider this to be of primary importance because it speaks not only to the ability of renewing African American congregations, but also of students developing skills that will translate into any context. The particularity of the class requires students to learn how to exegete hip-hop resources for the renewal of African American congregations. Students should walk away from the class with the ability to think historically, theologically, and ideologically about the cultures surrounding African American congregations.

Just as important, students who are not in African American contexts should be able to translate the skills they learn in this class to their context. The methodology is one that should translate to being able to exegete cultures in rural, suburban, etc., settings. This means that students are learning skills that will enable them to move from one context to another and be able to think about the appropriate resources for understanding that context. In

---

14. Talvacchia, *Critical Minds and Discerning Hearts*, 39.

addition to understanding the context, students will be able to do integrative work that uses the resources toward the renewal of the congregation.

One of the challenges to seminaries from many judicatory bodies is helping students to be more adaptive in their ministry settings. This class is structured for students to learn those skills and to be able to apply them in a variety of contexts. This form of learning is interdisciplinary because it pulls on what students have learned in Bible, theology, and contextual education. Ultimately this form of learning is what we hope the curriculum accomplishes at Saint Paul School of Theology because it prepares students for their ministry context by helping them to integrate what they learned from various disciplines.

## Considering a Theology of Pedagogy

I have been a hip-hop lover since first hearing "Rapper's Delight" in high school. I really started thinking about hip-hop differently when Scott La Rock was killed in 1987 by gun violence. Scott La Rock was a part of Boogie Down Productions with KRS-One, and after his death KRS-One really focused on socially conscious rap, e.g. "Stop the Violence." Because of Scott La Rock's death and KRS-One's commitment to make a difference, I began to understand the ways in which hip-hop culture was influencing African American youth and American culture in general.

In my second year of seminary, Tupac died (1996), and again I was reminded of how hip-hop culture mirrored African American culture. I also began to realize how theologically rich hip-hop rap was in interpreting Tupac in light of individuals like James Cone and Anthony Pinn. I started listening differently to rap and paying attention in new ways to hip-hop culture. It was also during seminary that womanist scholars like Katie Cannon helped me to see the ways in which hip-hop perpetuated androcentric cultural norms. It was in re-reading *Katie's Canon* a few years ago that a light bulb went off in terms of how I could think about hip-hop pedagogically.

I am indebted to Katie Cannon, who continues to inform my approach to pedagogy, and my approach in this class relies heavily upon her insights. She writes that "womanist pedagogy emerges out of this experience of Black Women challenging conventional and outmoded dominant theological resources, deconstructing ideologies that led us into complicity with our own oppression."[15] Obviously Cannon is focusing on womanist pedagogical

15. Cannon, *Katie's Canon*, 137.

Proleptic Pedagogy

approaches, but her ideas have relevance for my thinking about hip-hop. The idea of hip-hop as a valid theological resource challenges conventional theological material and even more liberative resources.

Cannon challenges us to consider our understanding of theological resources and to do so critically.[16] I am suggesting a similar move in dealing with hip-hop resources. As more scholars engage and use hip-hop as a theological resource, we have to develop the modes of inquiry that will define this genre of study. Cannon uses the image of three wheels that has stuck with me for years—wheel one is "traditional theological material, wheel two is African American cultural resources and wheel three is text by women."[17] Borrowing heavily from Cannon, I think about the wheels that inform a hip-hop pedagogy in the following way. Wheel one is African American theological resources which include black male and womanist thinking. Wheel two is African American ecclesial culture in its broadest dimensions. Wheel three is hip-hop resources that are often overlooked as having theological value and correlates to what Cannon does in reframing womanist thinking by doing the same for hip-hop resources.

Cannon has given me a road map for how to think about integrating hip-hop in the classroom and helping the students to integrate hip-hop into their contexts. In my re-visioning of the Cannon pedagogical model, the first wheel is African American theological resources. Individuals like Cannon have paved the way so that I can begin with African American theological resources and do not have to begin with more traditional resources. In the class we begin by reading Henry Mitchell and James Evans instead of having to validate the class by beginning with more traditional resources. This signals that we are able not only to engage our own history, but also to do so in a critical manner.

Beginning with theology from African American thinkers sets up a dialogue between those thinkers and the hip-hop resources. It is a dialogue similar to the one developed by individuals like James Cone and Cheryl Kirk-Duggan around spirituals and blues.[18] These thinkers help us to engage in a similar pedagogical praxis with hip-hop as they did with other African American resources. The goal is for students to see non-traditional resources like hip-hop as valid in the same way that the spirituals and blues at one time were considered non-traditional resources.

16. Ibid., 137–38.
17. Ibid., 138.
18. Cone, *Spirituals and Blues*; Cheryl Kirk-Duggan, *Exorcizing Evil*.

The second wheel is African American ecclesial culture in its broadest dimensions. By this I mean thinking about the role of the black church for those inside and outside of a particular congregation. I want students to think deeply about the impact of the black church on the broader culture. In the class I lecture on Lincoln and Mamiya's book, *The Black Church in the African American Experience*. The goal is to illustrate the way in which the black church shaped the culture and the culture shaped the black church. In terms of how we think about faith formation in the African American community, it is necessary to begin with an understanding of the black church.

To help students get a better grasp of the contribution of the black church I use a dialectical approach that analyzes the beginning of the seven historical African American denominations and the dis-ease that many in hip-hop culture have with the black church. The goal is to help students think concretely about the shifting culture in the African American community as it relates to faith formation taking place outside of the church.

The third wheel is a deep engagement with hip-hop resources. I begin every class with a particular hip-hop image, hip-hop rap, spoken word, etc. that speaks to the theological theme of class that day. My expectation is that students will analyze the hip-hop resource and make the connection to the theological theme, and as we move along during the semester understand the implications for faith formation. I am intentional in drawing diverse hip-hop resources like X-clan, Jay-Z, Kanye, Lil Kim, Lauryn Hill, and India Arie to name a few. The point is not to sanitize or force-feed certain hip-hop resources over others.

By using these various hip-hop resources, the goal is to help students to understand that hip-hop is not one dimensional—strictly rap music. Both those inside of the church and particularly the post-civil rights generations outside of the church are shaped by hip-hop culture. As public theologians we have to be able to analyze how individuals are being shaped by these resources and be able to engage critically these resources. The ability for students to do this creates what I believe are integrative thinkers.

My pedagogical approach to the class is shaped by Cannon. In particular, her image of the three wheels as I have envisioned them. I also seek to maintain the integrity of her womanist approach by making sure we critique the misogyny inherent in the culture. Obviously this is not the only critique of hip-hop culture, but one that needs to be highlighted. Notwithstanding the various critiques of hip-hop resources, the way I teach the class helps students to understand the importance of integrative thinking and its relevance for their context.

Proleptic Pedagogy

## Constructing a Pedagogical Proposal

The pedagogical method that grounds what takes place in the class is integrative thinking. By integrative thinking I mean the ability of students to hold together doctrinal ideas, cultural ideas and practices. Specific to this class it is holding together ecclesiology, hip-hop, and those practices that inform renewing African American congregations. Two main ideals have informed my conception of integrative thinking for this class and its implications for a teaching-learning community.

The first is addressing the issue of real life that continually pops up during seminary. Dorothy C. Bass and Miroslav Volf in their edited book, *Practicing Theology*, both begin their chapters with "But what does that have to do with real life?"[19] The implication is that seminary education is not practical or related to actual ministry. The problem with this, as Bass points out, is the separation of thinking from doing.[20] To think means action is not required and acting means no thought is necessary.

My concept of integrative thinking borrows from this problematic by addressing the question, "What are some cultural resources in tune with real life?" The answer is hip-hop culture because it speaks, depicts, and shapes culture in the United States. Methodologically having students to engage hip-hop culture puts them in direct contact with a resource that speaks to real life and particularly real African American life. Hip-hop culture is not the only way to do this, but it is a legitimate way of doing so.

The teaching learning community becomes a space where we encounter a lens for engaging that which is perceived as real. We not only engage it, but also begin to think about it theologically. It is the ability to think about hip-hop culture theologically that helps students to start integrating what they have learned with real life. For example, exploring why some hip-hop artists talk about God, but eschew African American congregations challenges students to figure out what is going on theologically in those artist's lives and what is missing theologically for those artists in African American congregations. Students begin the process of seeing how theology does in fact speak to real life and real life speaks to theology.

The second ideal is challenging students to think about what informs their practices of renewal. I believe this requires intentional theological reflection. I do differ, however, from some liberation models that promote an

---

19. Bass, "Introduction, 1; Volf, "Theology for a Way of Life," 245.
20. Bass, "Introduction," 6.

action-reflection-action model. I am in no way disparaging those models. What makes theological education unique is learning a language that allows you to do theological reflection. In other words, in order to reflect theologically on one's actions, a learned language to draw from is necessary. While this learned language does not have to be formal (seminary education), it still needs to be intentional. One has to be able to move from this learned language to appropriate actions in a particular setting.

Students not only have to be able to integrate theology and culture, but also engage critically their context to figure out appropriate renewal actions. In the class it is not enough to integrate ecclesiology with hip-hop culture: it is also necessary to articulate the practices needed to re-shape African American congregations as a part of the integration process. For example, a missional understanding of ecclesiology engages some in the hip-hop culture who are interested in urban renewal to consider some form of recycling as an appropriate practice in their ministry context. The point is students have to be able to integrate all of the components in way that authentically speaks to the theological content, cultural context, and ministry context.

I do believe, as we learn theological language and engage in various practices, we do need to reflect and change those practices as we move along. Reflecting on my example about a missional ecclesiology may lead to the insight that it would be more appropriate to start a community garden because vegetables are not readily available. My point is we do engage in reflection upon the practices, but this is possible because we have the language with which to do so. In the class it is helping students to draw upon this language in conjunction with the other components to engage in what I term integrative thinking.

In this essay I argue that utilizing hip-hop as a resource re-frames the way that students will consider and use theological material in their ministry contexts. They do this based upon the way I teach the class by drawing from various African American resources including hip-hop. They do this in the way that they learn to become listeners and not simply hearers. They do this in engaging a process of integrative thinking that helps to hold together theological ideals, cultural ideals, and appropriate practices for their ministry setting. While everyone may not use hip-hop, I believe the ideals behind this way of teaching, learning and integrating can be used in other settings.

# Bibliography

Adelizzi, Jane Utley. "The Artistry of Teaching and Learning." In *Educators, Therapists, and Artists on Reflective Practice*, edited by Julia J. Gentleman Byers and Michele Forinash, 12–23. New York: Lang, 2004.

Aleshire, Dan. "The Future Has Arrived: Changing Theological Education in a Changing World." Association of Theological Schools. Plenary Address at the ATS/COA Biennial Meeting, June 2010. Online: http://www.ats.edu/Resources/PublicationsPresentations/Pages/default.aspx.

Allen, Paula Gunn. *The Sacred Hoop: Recovering the Feminine in American Indian Traditions*. Boston: Beacon, 1986.

Anderson, Kenneth. "Changing Educational Paradigms," October 2010. Online: http://www.youtube.com/watch?v=zDZFcDGpL4U&list=FLfN5wJ2aJPBTj-ODyMWn-Qw &index=39&feature=plpp_video.

Ascough, Richard S. "Designing for Online Distance Education: Putting Pedagogy before Technology." *Teaching Theology and Religion* 5/1 (2005) 17–29.

Avery-Wall, Vanessa. "Engaging Difference: Exercises and Tips for Creating Experiential Learning Environments." *Modern Believing* 48/3 (2007) 36–50.

Banks, James A., Peter Cookson, Geneva Gay, Willis D. Hawley, Jacqueline Jordan Irvine, Sonia Nieto, Janet Ward Schofield, and Walter G. Stephan. "Diversity within Unity: Essential Principles for Teaching and Learning in a Multicultural Society." Seattle: University of Washington Center for Multicultural Education, 2000.

Barth, Karl. *Church Dogmatics*, IV/1, *The Doctrine of Reconciliation*. Edited by G. W. Bromiley and T. F. Torrance. Translated by G. W. Bromiley. Edinburgh: T. & T. Clark, 1956.

Bass, Dorothy C. "Introduction." In *Practicing Theology: Beliefs and Practices in Christian Life*, edited by Miroslav Volf and Dorothy Bass, 1–12. Grand Rapids: Eerdmans, 2002.

Betcher, Sharon V. *Spirit and the Politics of Disablement*. Minneapolis: Fortress, 2007.

Black Youth Project. Online: www.blackyouthproject.com.

Bozeman, Jean. "The Learning Community." In *Education for Christian Living: Strategies for Nurture Based on Biblical and Historical Foundations*, edited by Marvin L. Roloff, 59–72. Minneapolis: Augsburg, 1987.

*Bibliography*

Brewer, Joanna. "Pew Internet: Teens." Online: http://pewinternet.org/Commentary/2012/April/Pew-Internet-Teens.aspx.

Brookfield, Stephen D. *The Skillful Teacher*. San Francisco: Jossey-Bass, 1990.

Brookfield, Stephen D., and Stephen Preskill. *Discussion as a Way of Teaching: Tools and Techniques for Democratic Classrooms*. 2nd ed. San Francisco: Jossey-Bass, 2005.

Budde, Michael L., and Robert W. Brimlow. *Christianity Incorporated: How Big Business Is Buying the Church*. 2002. Reprinted, Eugene, OR: Wipf & Stock, 2007.

Caldwell, Elizabeth. "Religious Instruction: Homemaking." In *Mapping Christian Education: Approaches to Congregational Learning*, edited by Jack L. Seymour, 74–89. Nashville: Abingdon, 1997.

Cambiano, Renee L., Jack B. De Vore, and George S. Denny. "Learning Styles and Preferences Relating to Adult Students. *Academic Exchange Quarterly* 4/2 (2000) 41–49.

Cannon, Katie G. *Katie's Canon: Womanism and the Soul of the Black Community*. New York: Continuum, 1995.

Carder, Ken. "Market and Mission: Competing Visions for Transforming Ministry." Hickman Lecture, Duke Divinity School, October 16, 2001. Online: http://pulpitandpew.org.

Carmody, J. "Evolving Conceptions of Mindfulness in Clinical Settings. *Journal of Cognitive Psychotherapy* 23/3 (1991) 270–80.

Chávez, Alicia Fedelina, and Florence Guido-DeBrito. "Racial and Ethnic Identity and Development." *New Directions for Adult and Continuing Education* 84 (Winter 1999) 39–47.

Click, Emily. "Contextual Education." In *The Wiley-Blackwell Companion to Practical Theology*, edited by Bonnie J. Miller-McLemore, 347–56. New York: Blackwell, 2012.

Coburn, Thomas B. "The Convergence of Liberal Education and Contemplative Education—Inevitable?" In *Meditation and the Classroom: Contemplative Pedagogy for Religious Studies*, edited by Judith Simmer-Brown and Fran Grace, 3–12. Albany: SUNY Press, 2011.

Cone, James H. *The Spirituals and Blues: An Interpretation*. Maryknoll, NY: Orbis, 1992.

Delamarter, Steve, and Daniel L. Brunner. "Theological Education and Hybrid Models of Distance Education." *Theological Education* 40/2 (2005) 145–64.

D'Souza, Mario. "Theological Reflection and Field Based Learning for Religious Education." *Journal of Adult Theological Education* 6/1 (2009), quoting *Congregation for Catholic Education, Lay Catholics in Schools: Witnesses to Faith*. Rome, 1982. Article 16 81–97.

DuPaul, George J., Elizabeth A. Schaughency, Lisa L. Weyandt, Gail Tripp, Jeff Kiesner, Kenji Ota, and Heidy Stanish. "Self-Report of ADHD Symptoms in University Students: Cross-Gender and Cross-National Prevalence." *Journal of Learning Disabilities* 34 (2004) 370–79.

Eiesland, Nancy L. *The Disabled God: Toward a Liberatory Theology of Disability*. Nashville: Abingdon, 1994.

Ericsson Company. "Talking, Texting, Poking and Dating: How Teens are Using Technology in Their Social Lives." Online: www.ericsson.com/res/docs/2012/howteenagersareusingtechnologyintheirsociallives.pdf.

Erskine, Noel Leo. *Black Theology and Black Pedagogy*. NewYork: Palgrave Macmillan, 2008.

Fink, L. Dee. *Creating Significant Learning Experiences: An Integrated Approach to Designing College Courses*. San Francisco: Jossey-Bass, 2003.

## Bibliography

Foley, Edward. "Theological Reflection, Theology and Technology: When Baby Boomer Theologians Teach Generations X & Y." *Theological Education* 41/1 (2005) 45–56.

Foster, Charles R., Lisa E. Dahill, Lawrence A. Goleman, and Barbara Wang Tolentino. *Educating Clergy: Teaching Practices and Pastoral Imagination*. San Francisco: Jossey-Bass, 2006.

Foster, Dom David. *Reading with God: Lectio Divina*. New York: Continuum, 2006.

Freire, Paulo. *Pedagogy of the Oppressed*. Translated by Myra Bergman Ramos. New York: Herder & Herder, 1970.

French, J. R. P., and B. Raven. "The Bases of Social Power." In *Studies in Social Power*, edited by D. Cartwright, 150–67. Ann Arbor, MI: Institute for Social Research, 1959.

Freud, Sigmund. *Beyond the Pleasure Principle*. Seattle: Pacific Publishing Studio, 2010.

Friedman, Edwin. *A Failure of Nerve: Leadership in the Age of the Quick Fix*. Edited by Margaret M. Treadwell and Edward W. Beal. New York: Seabury, 2007.

———. *Generation to Generation: Family Process in Church and Synagogue*. New York: Guilford, 1985, 2011.

"The Future of Theological Education" (Issue Focus). *Theological Education* 46/2 (2011).

Gardner, Howard. *Multiple Intelligences: The Theory in Practice*. New York: Basic Books, 1993.

Gilligan, Carol, Janie Victoria Ward, and Jill McLean Taylor with Betty Bardige, editors. *Mapping the Moral Domain*. Cambridge: Harvard University Press, 1988.

Ginsberg, Margery B., and Raymond J. Wlodkowski. *Diversity and Motivation: Culturally Responsive Teaching in College*. 2nd ed. San Francisco: Jossey-Bass, 2009.

Guggenheim, Davis, director. *Waiting for "Superman."* Electric Kinney Films, Participant Media, and Walden Media, 2010.

Hall, Thelma, Sr. *Too Deep for Words: Rediscovering Lectio Divina*. Mahwah, NJ: Paulist, 1985, 1988.

Harris, Maria. *Teaching and Religious Imagination*. San Francisco: Harper & Row, 1987.

Harris, Maria, and Gabriel Moran. "Educating Persons." In *Mapping Christian Education*, edited by Jack Seymour, 58–73. Nashville: Abingdon, 1997.

Hess, Mary E. *Engaging Technology in Theological Education: All that We Can't Leave Behind*. The Communication, Culture, and Religion Series. Lanham, MD: Rowman & Littlefield, 2005.

———. "What Difference Does It Make?: Digital Technology in the Theological Classroom." *Theological Education* 41/1 (2005) 77–91.

Hess, Mary E., and Stephen D. Brookfield. "How Can We Teach Authentically? Reflective Practice in the Dialogical Classroom." In *Teaching Reflectively in Theological Contexts: Promises and Contradictions*, edited by Mary E. Hess and Stephen D. Brookfield, 18–38. Malabar, FL: Krieger, 2008.

hooks, bell. *Teaching to Transgress: Educating as the Practice of Freedom*. New York: Routledge, 1994.

Hough, Joseph C., and John B. Cobb. *Christian Identity and Theological Education*. Scholars Press Studies in Religious and Theological Scholarship. Chico, CA: Scholars, 1985.

Jay-Z, and Kanye West. "No Church in the Wild." Roo-A-Fella, Roc Nation, Def Jam, 2012. Online: http://www.youtube.com/watch?v=M37VucWho6Y.

Jewell, John P. "What Does All *This* Mean for the Church?" *Theological Education* 41/1 (2005) 17–31.

Johnston, D. Kay. "Adolescents' Solutions to Dilemmas in Fables: Two Moral Orientations—Two Problem Solving Strategies." In *Mapping the Moral Domain,* edited by Carol

## Bibliography

Gilligan, Janie Victoria Ward, and Jill McLean Taylor with Betty Bardige, 49–72. Cambridge: Harvard University Press, 1988.

Kerka, Sandra. "Adults with Learning Disabilities." ERIC Clearinghouse on Adult, Career, and Vocational Education. ERIC Digest 189. Online: http://www.ldonline.org/ld_indepth/adult/eric189.html.

Kirk-Duggan, Cheryl. *Exorcizing Evil: A Womanist Perspective on the Spirituals.* Bishop Henry McNeal Turner/Sojourner Truth Series in Black Religion 14. Maryknoll, NY: Orbis, 1997.

Kohut, Heinz. *The Analysis of the Self: A Systematic Approach to the Psychoanalytic Treatment of Narcissistic Personality Disorders.* New York: International Universities Press, 1971.

Langer, Ellen J. *The Power of Mindful Learning.* Cambridge, MA: Perseus Books, 1997.

Langer, Ellen J., and Mihnea Moldoveanu. "The Construct of Mindfulness." *Journal of Social Issues* 56/1 (2000) 1–9.

Lenhart, Amanda. "Teens, Smartphones and Texting." Online: http://pewinternet.org/Reports/2012/Teens-and-smartphones.aspx.

Lenhart, Amanda et al. "Social Media and Young Adults." Online: http://pewinternet.org/Reports/2010/Social-Media-and-Young-Adults.aspx.

Loder, James E., and W. Jim Neidhardt. *The Knights Move: The Relational Logic of the Spirit in Theology and Science.* Colorado Springs: Helmers & Howard, 1992.

Martin, Robert K. *The Incarnate Ground of Christian Faith: Toward a Christian Theological Epistemology for the Educational Ministry of the Church.* Lanham, MD: University Press of America, 1998.

———. "Theological Education in Epistemological Perspective: The Significance of Michael Polanyi's 'Personal Knowledge' for a Theological Orientation of Theological Education." *Teaching Theology and Religion* 1/3 (1998) 139–53.

Matthaei, Sondra Higgins. *Formation in Faith: Making Disciples in the Wesleyan Tradition* Nashville: Abingdon, 2000.

McFague, Sallie. *Models of God: Theology for an Ecological, Nuclear Age.* Philadelphia: Fortress, 1987.

Mercer, Joyce Ann. "Red Light Means Stop! Teaching Theology through Exposure Learning in Manila's Red Light District." *Teaching Theology and Religion* 5/2 (2002) 90–100.

Mezirow, Jack. *Fostering Critical Reflection in Adulthood: A Guide to Transformative and Emancipatory Learning.* San Francisco: Jossey-Bass, 1990.

Miglietti, Cynthia L., and C. Carney Strange. "Learning Styles, Classroom Environment Preferences, Teaching Styles, and Remedial Course Outcomes for Underprepared Adults at a Two-Year College." *Community College Review* 26/1 (1998) 1–15.

Mipham Rinpoche, Sakyong. "How to do Mindfulness Meditation." Online: http://www.shambhalasun.com.

Moltmann, Jürgen. "Liberate Yourselves by Accepting One Another." In *Human Disability and the Service of God: Reassessing Religious Practice,* edited by Nancy L. Eisland and Don E. Saliers, 105–22. Nashville: Abingdon, 1998.

Nieman, James R. *Knowing the Context: Frames, Tools, and Signs for Preaching.* Elements of Preaching. Minneapolis: Fortress, 2008.

Nouwen, Henri J. M. *Reaching Out: The Three Movements of the Spiritual Life.* Garden City, NY: Doubleday, 1975.

# Bibliography

Olson, Richard. "Genes, Environment, and the Components of the Reading Process." *Perspectives: International Dyslexia Association* 30/3 (2004) 6–9.

Paintner, Christine Valters, and Betsey Beckman. *Awakening the Creative Spirit: Bringing the Arts to Spiritual Direction.* New York: Morehouse, 2010.

Palmer, Parker J. *The Courage to Teach: Exploring the Inner Landscape of a Teacher's Life.* San Francisco: Jossey-Bass, 1998.

———. *To Know as We Are Known: A Spirituality of Education.* San Francisco: Harper & Row, 1983.

———. *To Know as We Are Known: A Spirituality of Education,* 2nd ed. San Francisco: HarperSanFrancisco, 1993.

———. *The Promise of Paradox: A Celebration of Contradictions in the Christian Life.* Notre Dame, IN: Ave Maria, 1980.

Polanyi, Michael. *Knowing and Being.* Edited by Marjorie Grene. Chicago: University of Chicago Press, 1969.

———. *Personal Knowledge: Towards a Post-Critical Philosophy.* Chicago: University of Chicago, 1962.

Polinska, Wioleta. "Engaging Religious Diversity: Towards a Pedagogy of Mindful Contemplation." *The International Journal of the Humanities* 9/1 (2011) 159–67.

Prensky, Marc. *Brain Gain: Technology and the Quest for Digital Wisdom.* New York: Palgrave, 2012.

———. "Digital Native, Digital Immigrants Part II: Do They Really *Think* Differently?" *On the Horizon* 9/6 (2001) 1–9.

———. "Digital Natives and Digital Immigrants." *On the Horizon* 9/5 (2001) 1–6.

———. *Teaching Digital Natives: Partnering for Real Learning.* Foreword by Stephen Heppell. Thousand Oaks: Corwin, 2010.

———. "Race and Ethnicity" (Issue Focus). *Theological Education* 45/1 (2009).

Reinders, Hans S. *Receiving the Gift of Friendship: Profound Disability.* Grand Rapids: Eerdmans, 2008.

Rendle, Gil. *Journey through the Wilderness: New Life for Mainline Churches.* Nashville: Abingdon, 2010.

Rideout, Victoria, et. al. *Generation M2:Media in the Lives of 8- to 18-Year-Olds.* A Kaiser Family Foundation Study. Menlo Park, CA: Henry J. Kaiser Family Foundation, 2010. Online: http://kaiserfamilyfoundation.files.wordpress.com/2013/04/8010.pdf.

Ritchhart, Ron, and David N. Perkins. "Life in the Mindful Classroom: Nurturing the Disposition of Mindfulness." *Journal of Social Issues* 56/1 (2000) 27–47.

Robinson, Sir Ken. "Changing Educational Paradigms" RSA, 6:56. Online: http://www.youtube.com/watch?v=zDZFcDGpL4U&list=FLfN5wJ2aJPBTj-ODyMWn-Qw&index=39&feature=plpp_video/.

Roozen, David A. "Educating Religious Leaders for a Multireligious World: Outcomes and Learning." *Theological Education* 47/1 (2012) 85–104.

Rosen, Larry D. *Rewired: Understanding the iGeneration and the Way they Learn.* New York: Palgrave Macmillan, 2010.

Russell, Letty M. *Church in the Round: Feminist Interpretation of the Church.* Louisville: Westminster John Knox, 1993.

———. *Growth in Partnership.* Philadelphia: Westminster, 1981.

Simmer-Brown, Judith, and Fran Grace. *Meditation and the Classroom: Contemplative Pedagogy for Religious Studies.* SUNY Series in Religious Studies. Albany: SUNY Press, 2011.

## Bibliography

Smith, Claire. "God's Neighborhood—Where Strangers Become Friends . . . and Family: a Guyanese Metaphor for Christian Education." Chicago: Association of Professors, Practitioners, and Researchers in Religious Education, 2003.

———. "To Follow Christ: Youth Ministry in a Technological Age." In *Youth Ministry in a Technological Age*, edited by Claire A. Smith and Sondra H. Matthaei, 1–13. Philadelphia: Xlibris, 2011.

Steinke, Peter L. *Congregational Leadership in Anxious Times: Being Calm and Courageous No Matter What*. Washington, DC: Alban Institute, 2006.

———. *How Your Church Family Works: Understanding Congregations as Emotional Systems*. Washington, DC: Alban Institute, 1993, 2006.

Stoddard, Tim. "Our Memories, Ourselves." *Bostonia* (Summer 2005) 10–15.

Stone, Linda. "Continuous Partial Attention." Online: http://lindastone.net/qa/continuous-partial-attention/

Sullivan, William M. "Introduction." In *Educating Clergy: Teaching Practices and Pastoral Imagination*, edited by Charles R. Foster, Lisa E. Dahill, Lawrence A. Golemon, and Barbara Want Tolentino, 1–16. San Francisco: Jossey-Bass, 2006.

Talvacchia, Kathleen T. "An Integrative Educational Strategy for Christian Leaders in a Multifaith World." *Teaching Theology and Religion* 9/2 (2006) 139–45.

———. *Critical Minds and Discerning Hearts: A Spirituality of Multicultural Teaching*. St. Louis: Chalice, 2003.

Tapscott, Don. *Grown Up Digital: How the Net Generation Is Changing Your World*. New York: McGraw-Hill, 2009.

"Technology and Educational Practices." *Theological Education* 41/1 (2005).

"Technology, Teaching, and Learning: Reports from the Field" (Issue Focus). *Theological Education* 42/2 (2007).

Teicher, Martin H. "Scars That Won't Heal: The Neurobiology of Child Abuse." *Scientific American* (March 2002) 68–75.

Thurman, Howard. *Jesus and the Disinherited*. 1949. Reprinted, Boston: Beacon, 1996.

Tisdell, Elizabeth J. *Exploring Spirituality and Culture in Adult and Higher Education*. San Francisco: Jossey-Bass, 2003.

Torrance, Thomas F., editor. *Theological Dialogue between Orthodox and Reformed Churches*. Vol. 1. Edinburgh: Scottish Academic, 1985.

Townes, Emilie M. "Response to: Appropriation and Reciprocity in Womanist/Mujerista/Feminist Work." *Journal of Feminist Studies in Religion* 8/2 (1992) 114–20.

Tuitt, Frank. "Realizing a More Inclusive Pedagogy." In *Race and Higher Education: Rethinking Pedagogy in Diverse College Classrooms*, edited by Annie Howell and Frank Tuitt, 243–65. Harvard Educational Review Reprint Series 36. Cambridge: Harvard Educational Review, 2003.

Volf, Miroslav. "Theology for a Way of Life." In *Practicing Theology. Beliefs and Practices in Christian Life*, edited by Miroslav Volf and Dorothy C. Bass, 245–63. Grand Rapids: Eerdmans, 2002.

Ware, Corine. *Discover Your Spiritual Type*. Washington DC: Alban Institute, 1995.

Ware, Kallistos (Bishop of Diokleia). "God Immanent Yet Transcendent: The Divine Energies according to Saint Gregory Palamas." In *In Whom We Live and Move and Have Our Being*, edited by Philip Clayton and Arthur Peacocke, 157–68. Grand Rapids: Eerdmans, 2004.

———. "Through Creation to the Creator." The Marco Pallis Memorial Lecture, 1995. London: Friends of the Centre, 1997.

*Bibliography*

Watkins, Ralph. *The Gospel Remix: Reaching the Hip Hop Generation*. Valley Forge, PA: Judson Press, 2007.
Weaver, Jace. "Native Americans and Religious Education." In *Multicultural Religious Education*, edited by Barbara Wilkerson, 256–90. Birmingham: Religious Education Press, 1997.
Webb-Mitchell, Brett. "Leaving Development Behind and Beginning Pilgrimage." *Religious Education* 96/1 (2001) 136–51.
Wesley, John. Sermon #2, "The Almost Christian" (1741). In *The Bicentennial Edition of the Works of John Wesley*, vol. 1: *Sermons 1–33*, edited by Albert C. Outler, 131–41. Nashville: Abingdon, 1984.
Wickett, Reg. "Adult Learning Theories and Theological Education." *Journal of Adult Theological Education* 2/2 (2005) 153–61.
Willcutt, Erik G., and Rebecca Gaffney-Brown. "The Etiology of Dyslexia, ADHD, and Related Difficulties: Using Genetic Methods to Understand Comorbidity." *Perspectives: International Dyslexia Association* (Summer 2004) 12–15.
Williams, Delores S. *Sisters in the Wilderness: The Challenge of Womanist God-Talk*. Maryknoll, NY: Orbis, 1993.

# Index

504 plans (accommodations), 11–12, 22

adaptive change, 33, 69; pedagogies, 15; work, 68–69
Adelizzi, Jane Utley, 63
Advanced Praxis Seminar, 8–12, 24, 26, 28, 92n1, 93- 95, 98, 106n32, 108, 110, 131n2
African American (or black), 94, 118; church/congregations/denomination, 130–33, 134n6, 135–36, 139–40; context, 13, 131–32, 136, 138; cultures, 114, 136–39; dialogue, 108; discrimination towards, 6, 107; experience, 10, 12–13, 93, 95, 101, 137, 139–40; literature, 104–5; perspectives, 130; portrayals of, 93; resources, 138, 141; scholars, 95; struggles, 96; students, 9, 12–13, 57n3, 95, 98, 132; white racial divide, 6, 13; youth, 137
Aleshire, Dan, 2–3
Allen, Paula Gunn, 118
anxiety/anxious, 27, 31–34, 38; climate of, 32; non-anxious, 38–39, 42, 49; systems, 32, 33; transitions, 26
appropriation, 101–2, 132
arts, 111, 120, 128
attentiveness, 51, 54, 88, 100, 126, 136
authentic community, 88; discipleship, 46; relationships, 83–84; spaces, 80; spirituality, 36

Avery-Wall, Vanessa, 36
authenticity, 80, 83, 99, 124–25
awareness, 4, 6, 21, 26, 38, 39, 40, 41n26, 49, 50, 54, 81, 89, 111, 113, 121–23, 126, 133; contemplative and analytical, 40, 42, 48; cultural, 17; social, 62n9; stable and non-reactive, 41

banking model of education, 19, 47, 109
baptism, 46, 48, 65
Barth, Karl, 45
Bass, Dorothy C., 140
Bozeman, Jean, 87
Brimlow, Robert W., 35
Brokenleg, Martin, 115, 116
Brookfield, Stephen D., 4, 7, 24, 40
Budde, Michael L., 35

Caldwell, Elizabeth, 86, 87
calling (to ministry/teaching), 30, 65–66, 67
Cannon, Katie G., 104, 134, 137, 138
Carder, Ken, 35
Carmody, J., 41
Chávez, Alicia Fedelina, 121
Christology, 45
church, 67–68, 70, 75, 86–87, 113, 118, 120, 131, 134; and big business, 35; as body of Christ, 45–46; calling, 66; challenges, 68–69; corporate model of, 44; future of, 59, 96, 123; growth, 33;

151

## Index

incarnational, 45, 50, 59, 70, 96–99, 109, 113, 117, 123–24; life, 31, 33, 44; mainline, 68; ministry, 41, 94; racism in, 98, 127; renewal of, 98, 121, 128; society/the world, 20, 45, 71, 96–97, 128; spiritual discipline, 54; and theological education, 1, 4, 7, 120

Class Participation Self-Evaluation, 22, 28
Click, Emily, 63, 69
Cobb, John B. Jr., 96, 97, 98
Coburn, Thomas B., 39
collaboration, 2, 25, 72, 80, 85, 88–89, 117, 127, 129
communion, 41–2, 45–46, 48, 54, 119
community, 1, 2, 5–6, 16, 44, 52–56, 60–61, 70, 78, 80–83, 86, 95, 97, 102, 107, 113, 115; Christian, 65–66, 78, 96, 119; classroom, 8, 13; face-to-face, 74, 77, 88; faith, 20, 119; global, 120, 128; hip-hop; 133, and identity, 117–18, 126; inclusive, 84; neighborhood, 84; synergy of, 20; teaching-learning, 10, 14, 16, 19–20, 22–24, 29, 53, 70–71, 74, 83, 87–89, 91, 95–96, 98, 102–4, 123, 126–27, 129, 140
Cone, James H., 138
congregational life, 30; alternative models of, 33; conventions of, 33; practices, 30; systems, 32
connectedness, connectivity, 74, 80, 81, 113, 116, 124
conscientization, 65, 136
consciousness, 30, 39, 41, 47–48, 51, 65
contemplative, 33, 38, 41, 49; awareness, 40, 42; discipline, 38, 43; mindfulness, 39, 41; prayer, 30, 38, 41, 50–51
context, 19, 29, 38, 40, 42, 64, 69, 87, 96, 98–100, 134, 136–39, 141; cultural, 2, 141; digital, 5; global, 97; ministry/congregational, 9, 13, 36, 95, 53, 70, 98, 123, 131,

137, 141; seminary/classroom, 5, 6, 13, 18, 21, 65, 81, 87, 90; social, 12, 99
contextual education, 10, 55, 57n3, 59, 60, 63, 66, 69, 128, 132, 137
course design, 1, 9, 12, 17, 21, 25, 26, 108
course management software, 2, 5, 9–10, 27, 71, 123; *see also* Moodle
creativity, 19–20, 26, 74n13, 88, 90, 94, 120, 128, 131
critical analysis, 116; engagement, 20, 33, 44, 74, 134–36, 139, 141; reflection, 63, 65, 99, 120, 125–26; thinking, 12, 16, 94, 103, 110
culture, 17–8, 40, 45, 80, 94, 101, 111, 113–14, 117–18, 120, 122, 124–27, 136–37, 139, 141; dominant, 15–18, 99, 124
cultural context, 141; awareness, 17; difference, 15, 56, 89, 113; environment, 62, 128; exegetes, 131–32, 136; expectations, 121; experience, 122; gaps, 59; heritage, 113; ideas, 140, 141; identity, 117, 120, 125; pluralism, 125; resources, 140; traditions, 118; way of reflecting, 112; wealth, 18
culturally relevant/responsive teaching/pedagogy, 15, 16, 18, 121, 124, 127
curriculum, 1–2, 10, 18, 31, 81, 90, 93, 119, 137

denominational/denominations, 35, 116; change, 34; decline, 2, 33; differences, 9; mainline, 34, 96; principles/traditions, 94, 114
dialogue, 24, 45, 62, 93, 102–4, 108, 123, 135–36, 138
digital age, 72–73, 77; classroom resources, 5, 70; expertise, 72; immigrants, 3, 5, 9, 14, 23, 72–73, 75; landscape, 76; language, 5, 72; natives, 3, 5, 9, 14, 23, 72–73,

77–78; resources, 90; world/media, 71, 74, 76
disciples/discipleship, 19–20, 29–31, 34, 36, 39, 46, 52, 58
discipline(s), 20, 38–43, 50–51, 54, 68, 70, 86, 94, 96–97, 119, 131
discussion (as teaching method), 12–13, 16, 22–23, 25, 27–28, 30, 37, 51–53, 60, 64, 77, 90, 102, 107, 109, 111–12, 119, 123, 125; asynchronous/synchronous, 23; online, 23–25, 91
divergent, thinkers, 111, 113–14, 119–22, 124, 126–28
diversity, 7, 31, 121, 128, 132; communities, 122; culture, 16, 113–4, 117, 120, 126; educational practices/learning experiences/pedagogical approaches, 2, 5–7, 108; experiences, 95; learning styles and ability, 3–6, 10, 14–15, 18, 21; peoples, 113–15, 118–21, 124, 126–28; racial/ ethnic, 10–11, 31, 56, 57n3, 59, 98, 110, 121–22, 124–25, 131; socioeconomic, 59; spirituality, 30; student body, 1–4, 8–10, 14–15, 17–18, 21, 25–26, 111, 113, 122–23, 132; technological, 5; theological perspectives/scholarship, 9, 15, 21n17, 95, 128; thinking, 120
divine action and engagement, 106; imagination, 19–20; life, 41, 46, 48–49, 54; model, 20; monarch, 44
D'Souza, Mario, 62

economic models, 44; needs, 67; situation, 57; status, 59
*Educating Clergy*, 4, 6–7, 61
education, 31, 52, 82–83; activities, 7; approach, 10; arena, 82; background and abilities, 6, 113; collaboration, 85; community, 83; decline, 34n8; environment, 31, 84, 121, 128; ethos, 78; experiences, 3; focus, 33; goals, 85; literature, 6, 17, 21; methods, 77; models, 2; paradigms, 120; practices, 2, 39; process, 52, 76, 83, 88, 90, 122; setting, 81; space, 79, 81–82, 84–85, 87–90; staff, 82; strategies, 73, 77; techniques, 9; technology, 3; theory, 39, 99, 119; transitions, 6
ego, 41–43, 51
engagement, 5, 6, 7, 13, 15, 20, 24, 31, 33, 36, 38–40, 49–50, 62–63, 71, 74, 89, 91, 93, 95, 99–101, 103, 107–8, 110, 114, 127, 128, 132, 133–34, 136, 138, 140–41; community/world, 60, 74–75, 77, 106, 120; engaged knowledge, 61, 108; ministries, 20; pedagogy, 15, 38, 61, 75, 98, 121, 133; student, 1, 3, 10–11, 14, 21, 24, 28, 37–38, 52, 56, 64, 66, 69, 75–79; theo-ethics, 104
"Engaging Local Ministries" (ELM), 59, 103, 109, 117, 125, 133, 135, 141
ethics, 93–6, 100; of justice, 116–17; of response and care 116–17
ethnicity, 1, 3, 4, 6, 9, 15–16, 21, 57–58, 63, 95, 98, 121, 127

face-to-face courses learning, 2, 23, 25, 70–72, 74–75, 77, 84, 88–91
facilitation, 22–23, 25, 62, 64–66, 69, 79, 87–89, 95–96, 98–99, 107, 110
fear, 10, 38, 57n4, 58–59, 61, 80, 90, 108
financial resources, 2, 15, 35, 127–28
Fink, L. Dee, 108, 109, 110
Foley, Edward, 75
formation, 38, 40, 55, 59, 61–64, 71, 94, 96, 99–100, 118–19, 139
Freire, Paulo, 47
French, J. R. P., 34
Freud, Sigmund, 42
Friedman, Edwin, 32–33

Gilligan, Carol, 116
Ginsberg, Margery B., 15–19

*Index*

Grace, Fran, 39
Guido-DiBrito, Florence, 121

Hall, Thelma, 50
Harris, Maria, 81, 119
Hess, Mary E., 7, 40, 72, 73, 76, 78
hooks, bell, 100, 101, 102, 103
Hough, Joseph C., 96, 97, 98
Howell, Nancy R., 92, 93, 94, 106
Hubbard, Laura, 21, 27
hybrid courses and learning, 2, 71, 128
*han*, 13, 96
hip-hop, attire in, 134–35; critiques of, 139–40; culture, 132–35, 137, 139–141; engaging, 130, 132–36, 138–41; misogyny in, 132, 140; pedagogy, 138; profanity in, 134; resources, 130–33, 135–36, 138–39, 141
holism, 10, 14, 38, 41, 47, 94, 99, 101, 104–5, 109–10, 115, 117, 131
hospitality, 6, 12, 25, 36, 54, 79–80, 82–84, 88, 113, 120, 123–25, 128; classroom/learning, 15–17, 21, 79, 114, 117, 126

identity, 4, 6, 13, 21n17, 29, 33, 35–37, 53–54, 81, 88, 113, 116, 118–19, 124–25; Christian, 2, 85, 96–97; cultural, 17, 45, 47, 117, 120; racial/ethnic, 99, 121; seminary, 1; sexual, 1–2, 95; spiritual, 31
ideologies, 34, 40, 136–37
immigration, 13, 56–57, 96
incarnation, 29, 37, 38, 43, 45–49, 54; epistemology, 47n36, 47–48, 54; model, 44–5; proleptic, 46; theological education, 47; theology, 49, 51
institution, 21, 32, 35, 68; decline, 34; growth, 31, 35–37; process, 12; support, 128; viability, 31
integration, 9–10, 23–24, 65, 76, 81, 87, 91–92, 97, 99, 100–4, 107–9, 110, 119, 129, 133, 137–38
integrative thinking, 28, 94–95, 98–100, 109, 132, 141

integrity, 22, 35, 41, 86, 99, 101, 105, 110–15, 139–40; ethics, 131; of learning sequence, 12

Jewell, John P., 7
Johnston, D. Kay, 117
Kirk-Dugan, Cheryl, 138
Kohut, Heinz, 42
Korea, 29, 32; context, 33; experience, 13; students, 12, 29, 32, 57n3, 58n6, 95, 98, 132

Langer, Ellen J., 39
Latino/a/Hispanic context, 57n3, 57–58, 96; culture 118; students, 12, 18, 95, 98
leadership, 13, 19, 30, 32–34, 46, 52, 58; Christ-like/Christian, 31, 42, 45, 52; church 31–32, 34–35, 37, 43–45, 50, 95, 97–98, 113, 117, 119, 123–24; as command and control, 44; course, 50–51; development/education, 2, 7, 70, 128; effective, 34; ministerial, 33, 35, 36, 44, 46, 61, 95; model of, 33; skills, 41, 96
learning, 3–5, 9–11, 13–15, 18, 20–23, 25–26, 37, 40, 47, 48n39, 51–53, 55–56, 59, 61, 78–79, 82–83, 86–90, 99, 101, 108, 113, 117, 121, 124–27, 129, 131, 136, 141; accommodations, 12; approaches, 10–11, 17–18, 63, 76–77; climate, 19, 22–23; collaborative, 19, 129; community, 2, 10, 14, 16, 19–20, 22–24, 53–54, 60, 78, 95–96, 98, 103–4, 109, 123, 140; consciousness in the act of, 47; contexts, 15, 58, 76; disabilities, 2, 3, 6, 9, 11, 12, 14–15, 21–22, 24; disability statement, 22; experience/experiential, 5–7, 10, 55, 59, 61, 63–66, 69, 85, 89, 95, 98, 108–10; exposure, 62, 64; interdisciplinary, 109, 137; life-long, 14, 18, 20; locations, 56–58, 60–61, 66–67, 69; multiple modes of, 23; needs, 20;

non-traditional, 15; outcome, 133; styles/strategies, 2, 4, 5; transformative,18, 63–65, 69
learning environments, 4–6, 8, 10, 16–19, 21, 99, 100, 121; hospitable, 21, 54; inclusive, 6; pluralistic, 10, 18
Learning Styles/Learning Disabilities Course Inventory, 21, 26–27
Listening, 13, 25, 27, 36, 39, 41, 51, 57, 60, 66, 89, 95, 100–102, 106–7, 110, 115, 126–27, 132–33, 141
*logos,* 45–46
mainline denominations, 29, 32, 34, 68, 96

Martin, Robert K., 47, 54
Matthaei, Sondra H., 111, 119
McFague, Sallie, 44
mentoring, 24–25, 41, 62, 63, 75
Mercer, Joyce Ann, 60, 62, 63, 64, 65
Mezirow, Jack, 65
mindfulness/mindful pedagogy, 38–41, 48–49, 51, 54, 89, 100, 102, 110
ministry, contexts, 36, 53, 131, 137, 141; practices, 44, 53, 57, 119–21, 129, 141; setting, 25, 94, 96, 98, 107, 131–37, 141
"Ministry in Context," 55, 63–65, 69
Moldoveanu, Mihnea, 39
Moodle, 5, 10–11, 27–28, 71
monarchical model of God, 43–44
Moss, Jami, 111, 112, 121, 129
multiculturalism, 18, 98–99, 113, 122, 124, 127
multiple intelligences, 6, 11

Native American context, 112n2, 114, 119; cultures, 113–18, 127; students, 12, 95, 98, 113, 127–28
neighborhood, 79–84, 91
net generation, 71, 73, 77
Nieman, James R., 57
Nouwen, Henri J. M., 80

objectification, 29, 31, 33, 36, 54

"other," 13, 20, 29, 31, 36, 38, 41–42, 48, 56–57, 59, 66–67, 81–82, 86, 99, 104, 110, 122, 126, 132, 136

Palmer, Parker J., 41, 83, 126
partnership, 72, 81, 85, 88–89, 98, 100
pedagogical agility, 9, 10, 19, 21, 26; approaches, 4, 7, 74, 98–100, 108, 110, 132, 137–38; challenge(s), 3, 5, 6, 9–13, 59, 94–95, 131–33; concerns, 16; consequence, 17; conversations, 7; development, 3, 114; expertise, 14; flexibility, 25–26; innovation, 15; issue, 61, 131; movements, 26; proposal, 67, 110; repertoire, 9; responsiveness, 15–16; resources, 14; skill, 7, 14, 17; strategies, 1, 3–5, 8, 15, 25, 73, 95, 99, 101–4, 132–33
pedagogy, 3–5, 9, 11, 19, 51, 71, 74, 96, 107–8, 113–17, 120–21, 123–24, 137; adaptive, 15; approach, 19, 137; contemplative, 49; culturally hospitable, 122–29; empowering, 14; engaged, 100–102, 105; hip-hop, 138; incarnational, 54; of natural selection, 13; over-involved, 14; of protection, 13; replacement, 17; theological, 20, 38, 40, 123, 131; theological framework for, 7, 19–20, 38, 65, 105
Perkins, David N., 39, 40
Polanyi, Michael, 47–8
Polinska, Wioleta, 38, 40
Powe. F. Douglas Jr., 92, 93, 94, 106, 130, 134
practice of justice, 106–8
pragmatic, 33, 40, 51, 53, 95; professionalism, 34, 36–38, 49, 51–52, 54
praxis, 3, 86, 93, 95, 107, 110, 119–20, 131, 138; insight, 13
Prensky, Marc, 5, 72, 73, 76, 77, 78, 79
Preskill, Stephen, 24

*Index*

privilege/white, 5, 16–17, 44, 60, 67, 93–94, 96–98, 100, 107–8, 110, 122
professional formation, 2–4, 6–7, 10, 20, 23–6, 94, 98–99, 110
proleptic pedagogy, 10, 26, 46–48, 54, 71

racial challenges/tensions, 12; reconciliation, 108
racism, 6, 92, 94–95, 98, 106
Raven, B., 34
relationship, 19–20, 27–28, 35, 57, 62, 65, 67, 72, 76, 79–81, 83, 85–86, 99, 109–10, 116, 119, 126
Rendle, Gil, 68, 69
renewal, 36, 53–54, 66, 96, 98, 131–32, 136–7, 140–1
resistance, 59, 61, 63–64, 106
revelation, 45, 114–15
Ritchhart, Ron, 39, 40
Rinpoche, Mipham, 41
Robinson, Ken, 120
Rosen, Larry D., 73, 77
Russell, Letty M., 81, 82, 85

self, 42, 13, 43, 48–51, 80, 99, 110, 121, 126; expanding centeredness, 43; self-awareness, 16, 26, 99, 122, 124, self-determination, 118; self-exploration, 33; self-expression, 123; self-identification, 13
Simmer-Brown, Judith, 61–62
small group, 23, 27, 30, 52, 56, 58, 66, 89, 123
Smith, Claire Annelise, 73, 77
spirituality, 19, 20, 33, 35–36, 38, 40–41, 53–54, 58, 67, 70, 88–89, 95, 98–99, 100–107, 110, 119, 124–25, 127–28; diversity, 30; health, 52–53; identity, 31; orientation, 15; sense-making, 30; spiritual direction, 111, 125; typology, 30
spirituals and blues, 138
Steinke, Peter L., 33
Stone, Linda, 74

syllabus, 8, 21–23, 26, 28, 85, 93–94, 102–3, 106, 131

Talvacchia, Kathleen T., 36, 38, 54, 98, 99, 122, 124, 134, 136
Tapscott, Don, 73
teaching, 5–7, 12, 14–5, 17, 20–24, 26, 33, 37, 44–45, 47, 53, 59, 63, 66, 76–78, 81, 85, 87, 89, 91, 95, 97, 100, 106, 108, 113, 114, 117, 121, 124–27, 131, 141; approaches, 10–11, 63; authenticity, 40; community, 14, 103–4; critically responsive, 2, 4, 15–16, 18; future of, 10; learning environment, 8, 16–18, 98, 140; multicultural, 99, 124; strategies, 3, 5, 108–9, 122
technology, 4–5, 7, 10, 23, 71–3, 88, 90, 128; changes in, 11; classroom, 1–3, 9, 14, 71, 75; contemporary, 74–80, 84; offsite, 71; purpose and philosophy of, 74; technophobia, 5
*theos*, 40
theological education, 3–5, 7, 14–5, 18–21, 24, 26, 31, 33, 36–38, 41, 43, 49, 54, 61–63, 69, 72, 74–79, 84–85, 87–88, 96–97, 99–100, 107, 109, 117, 119–20, 126, 128, 141; challenge, 9, 10; changes in, 1–3; concern, 7, 94; content/context of, 6, 65, 74, 81, 120; conversations/dialogue, 93, 102–4; for diverse people, 113, 115–16, 121; as formation, 10, 19–20, 40; future of, 3, 10; incarnational/sacramental, 47–48; purpose of, 23; schools, 3
theology, 94, anthropology, 76; approaches, 10, 46; convictions, 64, 66–67; development, 74; imagination, 20; questions, 25, 78; reflection, 7, 20, 21n17, 25, 62, 70–71, 78, 92, 95, 100, 106–7, 110, 140; resources, 131, 133, 137–38; struggles, 24; understanding, 66

*Index*

theology, Black/Womanist, 12, 24–25, 93, 95, 98, 100, 103, 104, 138; and race, 9, 12; white, 13, 95
"Theology in Black and White," 8, 26, 28, 92–95, 100, 102–3, 105n27, 106, 131; theology as a way of life, 98, 104–5, 107, 110
thought, analytical, 117; divergent, global, 117; "heart," 115; linear, 116; relational, 116
"third disestablishment," 68
Tisdell, Elizabeth J., 124, 125
Torrance, Thomas F., 45
Townes, Emilie M., 102, 107, 131, 132, 133
transformation, 3, 19, 20, 34, 41, 54, 56, 58, 64–65, 83, 98–99, 110, 112, 116, 125, 128; personal and social, 38; redemptive, 48–49
transgressing boundaries, 100, 102–3
truth-telling, 107–8
Tuitt, Frank, 121, 122, 123

videoconference/videoconferencing, 2, 9, 5, 11, 23

vision, 32, 34–35, 67, 99, 105, 109, 114–15, 119, 128–29
vocation, 6, 31, 35–36, 52–53, 65–66, 70, 110, 124, 126
Volf, Miroslav, 105, 106, 140

Ware, Corine, 30
Ware, Kallistos, 46
Watkins, Ralph, 135
Weaver, Jace, 114, 116
Webb-Mitchell, Brett, 118, 119
Wesley, John, 126
Wesleyan thought, 13, 119, 126
Western European model, 113–14, 116, 118, 128
whiteness, normative, 93
Wickett, Reg, 63, 64, 65
Wlodkowski, Raymond J., 15–19
worldview 13, 34, 100, 113–15, 134

*you*Theology, 70, 71, 73, 75, 77, 82, 88–90
youth/adolescents, 71, 88, 117, 137

157

www.ingramcontent.com/pod-product-compliance
Lightning Source LLC
Chambersburg PA
CBHW030859170426
43193CB00009BA/666